# Auld Lang Syne!

# Auld Lang Syne!
## Reliving Your Scottish Childhood!

Allan Morrison

ILLUSTRATED BY

*Besley*

www.nwp.co.uk

The Vital Spark is an imprint of
Neil Wilson Publishing Ltd
Suite Ex 8, Pentagon Centre
44 Washington Street
GLASGOW
G3 8AZ

Tel: 0141 221 1117
Fax: 0141 221 5363
E-mail: info@nwp.co.uk
http://www.nwp.co.uk

ACKNOWLEDGEMENTS
With grateful thanks to Alex and May Brown,
Jim Crumlish, Andrew Pearson, Ron and Anne Sheridan,
the Stevenson family, Morag and John Wilson and
also to Archie Wilson.

A catalogue record for this book is available
from the British Library.

10-digit ISBN: 1-903238-44-7
13-digit ISBN: 978-1-903238-44-8

Typeset in Slimbach
Designed by Mark Blackadder

Printed by Biddles.

# INTRODUCTION

Take a wee journey back to a more innocent time when the world
was a safer, saner place, where we enjoyed a much simpler lifestyle
and when our present hi-tech world seemed light years away. All you
have to do is dip into *Auld Lang Syne!* and celebrate this wonderful
compilation of long-forgotten memories. It's a simple trip as every
item is listed on an A-Z basis so you can hop on at any point and get
off whenever you feel like it.

Wallow in the past riches and
memorabilia of a Scottish childhood,
your very own treasure house of
memories; a time of wonder, fun and
youthful passion. There was nothing
quite like it. Today's Scottish child
may be able to load a DVD and play
on a PSP but, I ask you, can any of
them play peever beds?

We all have a nostalgic fondness for the past, for the things that
made us what we are. This is a record of our recent heritage, unique
to the land of Scotland, to days when strong character was formed,
often in difficult times. It can all come back to you at any moment in
a number of ways – perhaps a chance meeting with an old friend, a
glance at a photograph, or even by a scent. Then you find yourself
with a sentimental tear in the corner of your eye for a distant
memory of your youth. After all, your memories made you the
person you are.

This book is a rich tapestry of yesteryear, a profusion of youthful
interests that hopefully will take you for an emotional stroll down
your very own 'memory lane'.

Allan Morrison,
Gourock, December 2006

## ABC Minors

A cinema show for children on Saturday mornings where you could watch films about Flash Gordon, Tom Mix, The Bowery Boys, The Durango Kid, Hopalong Cassidy, Buck Jones and the Three Stooges etc. When it was your birthday, you were called up to the stage and everyone sang 'Happy Birthday' to you. In addition, each week all the boys and girls sang the ABC minors' song to the tune of 'Blaze Away'.

*We are the boys and girls well known,*
*As minors of the ABC.*
*And every Saturday we line up*
*To see films we like and shoot around with glee,*
*We love to laugh and have a singsong.*
*Such a happy crowd are we.*
*We're all pals together,*
*The minors of the ABC.*

## accordions

Joining up old tram or bus tickets to form an 'accordion' shape. Sometimes the 'accordion' would just keep on growing as you continually added to it.

## 'ages with'

Someone who 'ages with' someone else is the same age as that person. 'Ah'm ages with him.' Age seemed especially important in childhood. 'I'm seven and three quarters.' or 'She's just six and a half'. It is said that once you get beyond 85 you revert to using parts of a year when talking about age (a second childhood perhaps?).

### air-raid wardens

Responsible for sounding the air-raid sirens, putting out fires from incendiary bombs and ensuring the wartime blackout was maintained. A lot of fathers and sons who were not away fighting were air-raid wardens.

### aniseed balls

Small, hard-boiled sweets with a strong aniseed flavour. You bought the sweets in a wee poke (paper bag) and got a rare long sook out of them.

### apple, orange and a shiny new penny

Traditional at Christmas. These were in your stocking ... if you were lucky!

### Arbroath smokies

Perhaps the breakfast you had on a Sunday morning. A strong taste for a child and one that 'lingers' all day. A smokie is a small haddock cured with salt and then smoked on a spit over a fire (but only in Arbroath!).

### ashet

The shallow, oval serving dish used for home-made steak pies. Even now, can you smell your mother's steak pie?

### Atholl brose

Sweet oatmeal dessert made with cream, honey and whisky. If you got this at home you were really posh!

### aumrie

The larder, pantry or press where the food was kept. Before the days of fridges your mother had to shop each day to try and get fresh food.

### auntie beeny

An old lady you knew who dressed in the style of long ago, refusing to change even though the world of fashion and styles had moved on.

# B

## back green/court/drying green

If you lived in a tenement, you probably played in the back court of the building on a communal grassy or paved area, sometimes called a 'backie'. You spent a lot of your time here, sometimes much to the annoyance of neighbours who had put washing out to dry.

## baffle walls

Erected four feet away from the close mouths of tenements, just parallel with the pavement, these were solid brick walls, some six feet high, six feet wide and two feet thick, designed to deflect a bomb blast from a close mouth in case people were sheltering there. Some baffle walls were constructed of corrugated iron sheets held together by a frame and filled with sand. Needless to say the braver children used them as a climbing frame!

## bahookie

What you landed on when you fell. Your bottom! A combination of the word behind and *hough*, the Scots word for thigh. You might be told to 'Sit on yer bahookie and no' another word oot o' you!'

## bauldy bayne

The cheeky name you gave to someone who was bald. Children can be cruel!

## ball-bearings

Used for playing marbles: depending on its size it was deemed a 'tenner' or a 'twentier', meaning that your opponent had to hit it that number of times before they won the marble. Sometimes a glass marble would split when hit by one of these 'monsters'.

## ballies

These used to be seen in some high-street shops. They were round shells into which your bill and money were put by the assistant, then they whizzed away on an overhead rail to a central cash desk. Eventually they whizzed back with the receipt and change. Great entertainment!

## balls

Remember bouncing ('stoating') balls off a wall? You were probably in the playground. You had a routine to follow: first leg, second leg, legs together with the ball bouncing through from behind and 'big birly', the final bounce against the wall. Or it could be 'plainy, clappy, rolly pin, two-backy, right hand, left hand, high skitush, low skitush, turn yer back and away ye go, birly oh'. Alternatively, you recited, 'Archiball, ball, ball, King of the Jews, Jews, Jews, bought his wife some shoes'. Or perhaps the chant, 'The Old Grey Mare'.

## ballycog

The pail used to hold milk, either from a farm or from the milk cart that came around the streets. You had to ensure that not a drop was spilled on the way back otherwise you might get a clip round the lughole!

ballycog

## Band of Hope

This was a temperance organisation for children. It was founded in 1847 and was popular up until the 1960s. Children were requested to sign the pledge against the demon drink so that they would not fall into the ways of grown-ups.

*I swear by Almighty God to abstain from all intixico- all intaxi - all antixi -*

'I swear by Almighty God to abstain from all intoxicating liquors as beverages. Lord help me to keep this pledge'.

You were also asked to sing:

*Dare to be a Daniel,*
*Dare to stand alone.*
*Dare to pass a public house*
*And take your money home.*

**Band of Hope**

But I suspect that not all of the children signing the pledge kept their promise!

## bandstands

Some still exist but it was common to have them in parks where local bands and choirs performed, mostly on Sunday afternoons. Great places to play a variety of games.

## bannocks

These were biscuits, scones, barley-meal cake or an oatcake, depending on which part of the country you lived and probably home-baked on a griddle by your mother or grandmother. A freshly-baked bannock ... heaven!

## bare feet

Remember when all the summer holidays seemed to be hot? Remember running around in bare feet during the summer? Remember when the tar melted and bubbled on the roads? Why does in hardly ever happen now?

## battleships

The game where you and a friend drew small battleships on either end of a piece of paper. Then, with a pen or pencil, you quickly took turns in scrawling the pen across the page to see if you could hit the opposition navy. Caused many an argument and in its modern form is available in a properly manufactured way.

## batters on your school jotters

It was a requirement that your school jotters (exercise books) were covered to keep them clean. There were a variety of coverings used ranging from plain brown paper, wallpaper or just the local newspaper. 'Ah see you've the sports news on the front of your jotter, Morrison!'

## bauchle

A type of shapeless or worn-out shoe, often, by extension, used to describe a worn-out, useless or clumsy person who, if small in stature, would invariably be referred to as a 'wee bauchle'.

## baur

A funny story or joke you swapped with your pals. Hopefully, not too risqué!

## bawbee

This used to be an old Scots coin worth a ha'penny sterling, or sixpence in old Scots money. If you were lucky you got a couple of 'bawbees' as pocket money, though it has long since been out of circulation. Really the word was used to describe a small amount of money, such as: 'It's no' worth a wee bawbee'. The original bawbee was made of silver and named after the 16th-century Scottish mintmaster, Alexander Orrock of Sillebawby.

## beastie

A wee animal, spider, insect or 'creepy-crawlie'. Lots of them were quite scary depending on your age!

beastie

# beds

This was predominantly a game for girls with a bed of numbers and squares chalked onto the surface of the playground or pavement. These were numbered from 1, the start and finish, to 10, the turn and rest. Many of the beds resembled the outline of an aeroplane, with wings and a central 'fuselage'. A peever (a piece of marble, or a smooth stone, or an empty tin with a weight inside) was shuffled with the side of your foot, in a sort of hopping action across the boxes without putting both feet on the ground or allowing the peever to stop on a line. If you did so you were 'out' and someone else tried. When it was your turn again you had to start on the last number you landed on, but you had to shuffle the peever from the starting box onto that number before you could begin.

## besom

Cheeky wee besoms were female upstarts. 'You're a cheeky wee besom!' was the phrase often used to describe girls when they misbehaved. Usually the wee besoms were also 'nippy sweeties', that is, they had sharp tongues.

## best room

Many homes had a 'best room' or 'good room', where all the best furniture was. It was only for the use of a visitor, e.g. the minister, priest or doctor. Your mother would proudly 'protect' her best room, with the family only allowed in on very special occasions. 'And don't you dare touch anything,' she would say.

## bield

A wee shelter or gang hut you made with your pals. Probably made with wood and old lino. A secret place for an illicit cigarette?

## 'big hoose'

The largest house on a country estate or in a rural village. The local laird or factor would probably live there. Perhaps some of your family had a job there?

## bing

A large mound of waste, perhaps from a mine, that you may have played on against your parents' instructions!

### birdie's een

Tapioca, a hated pudding at school dinners; also called frogs' eggs. It comes from the cassava plant. Some children swore they would never eat the stuff again for the rest of their lives!

### 'birds and bees'

Scottish parents were often too embarrassed to talk to their children about such matters. Can you remember how and when you learned about the 'birds and the bees'?

### black-affronted

When ashamed, mortified or embarrassed you always said, 'I'm black-affronted.' And if you caused a problem that everybody knew about, your mother would say that she was 'black-affronted'.

birds and bees

### black bun

The fruitcake you had at New Year. It's very rich, moist and has a shortcake pastry base. Too much and you would get a sore stomach.

### black marias

The police van which had separate locked cubicles and was used to transport people to the police station, usually drunks on a Friday or Saturday night. Everybody stopped and looked as the black maria went past, wondering who had been 'lifted'.

### blate at the learning

If you were a bit shy, slow and timid at school, this might have been the way you were described.

### blatherskate

A babbler, someone who always talked nonsense. A real blether. You know them!

### blin' bargain

When you had to guess at something, or bought or exchanged a 'pig in a poke'. Boys and girls were forever swapping cigarette cards or scraps.

### blin' lump

A swelling or boil that never quite came to a head.

blatherskate

### blotting paper

Remember using blotting paper at school when you had put too much ink on the nib? Remember the daft boys who got balls of blotting paper, soaked them in ink, and threw them around?

### 'blowie'

A game played with cigarette cards. You laid them on the pavement against a wall, blew them, and if they turned over you won and you got the opponent's card. You also got dirty knees!

### blow football

Played on a table top with the players blowing through small plastic pipes to try to score goals. The ball was almost impossible to control but it was much cheaper than Subbuteo.

## blown-ups

An old-fashioned football made of leather panels with an inflatable bladder inside. Almost lethal if you headed it on a wet day especially if you came into contact with the lace. It had to be treated with Dubbin to keep it watertight.

## blue bags

These were the wee blue twist-bags of salt found in Smiths crisp packets so that you could choose how much to salt your own crisps.

blown·ups

You had to make sure you found it first, otherwise you suddenly found yourself crunching salt.

## bogies

Sometimes referred to as 'cairties', 'guidies', 'buggies' or 'pilers'. Little carts made out of the wheels of prams and wooden boxes.

People who had completed their family were always under pressure to give up the old pram so that a bogie could be made out of it. Normally a plank of wood was placed between the two axles, with a piece of rope used to steer the front wheels. 'Executive' models had a wooden handle as a brake!

## boilings

Coloured hard sweets made from sugar in a variety of flavours such as orange, lemon, lime or strawberry. Friends and relatives carried them in their pockets, and often gave you a boiling to 'sook' when you met them in the street. If it wasn't a boiling then it would definitely be a pan drop, the hard, round, mint, sweet.

## bomb shelters

There were various bomb shelters erected in areas of the country liable to come under German bombing. The Anderson shelter was called after the Home Secretary in 1938, John Anderson. It consisted of 14 sheets of corrugated iron, and was buried to a depth of four feet and then covered with 15 inches of soil. Only those with gardens benefited from the erection of this shelter.

## bombies

Sites flattened by German bombing during the Second World War and used as playgrounds by children. Sometimes if there had been a tenement on the site, digging took place to get out any coal remaining in the cellars. Games were played in the rubble, mostly jumping from one heap of stones to the next. It seemed years before these ruins were tidied up and cleared away.

## book and a skate

Children used to place a book on a roller skate then sit on it before hurtling down a sloping pavement. This always ruined your shoes, as you had to use your heels to brake. Not approved of by hard-up parents who, after having bought you a new pair of shoes, told you to 'take longer strides' to save the soles.

## bookies' runners

These men hung about closes and corners waiting to take bets to place with an illegal bookmaker. Sometimes your father might tell you to take his line and shilling to the local runner.

## booking/bottling/creeling

The pre-wedding ritual where a bride-to-be would be dressed up in silly, outlandish clothes such as net curtains and have to hold a cauliflower or turnip, then be paraded through the street by her female friends, followed by a long line of laughing children. She had to kiss as many men as possible, and if she kissed someone in uniform it was reputed to bring her good luck. On the other hand, the groom might suffer a worse fate: 'blackening', when he would be stripped naked, and mud, or worse, was smeared on his body. Enough to put you off getting married!

## bools (marbles)

Boys always had a pocketful of wee bools (balls) either made of glass (a 'glessy'), marble, or a 'jaurie', an earthenware marble. You took turns at trying to hit your opponent's marble, and if you did, it became yours.

## bouffant hairdos

Popular back-combed hairstyle, lifted high to form a beehive shape. At one time all the girls were into it.

**bouffant hairdo**

## bowie

The small tub which held sticks for the fire. You could buy bundles of sticks at the local shop and these would be put in the bowie ready for the next kindling.

## brambles

Collecting brambles in autumn to make jam was, and still is, a favourite pastime. To go 'bramblin' is to go berry picking. It was a popular family pastime collecting the berries in jars or tins with a little competition creeping in to see who could pick the most. Of course, some were eaten as you went along, especially the large, black, juicy ones!

## bread and dripping

Slices of bread dipped in hot dripping. Yech!

## bread poultices

These were placed hot on your chest to 'draw' an infection out before the days of antibiotics. Sometimes camphorated oil on a warmed flannel was also used. Mustard poultices were also popular but the smell stayed with you for days. A case of the cure being worse than the illness?

## bree

The broth your granny made, or in some cases, the way in which something was cooked. Granny's broth was always the best, especially the day after she had made it.

## breeks

Old-fashioned name for trousers. It is said that poor children often had holes in their breeks while richer children had patched holes in their breeks!

## bridie

A semi-circular pie with flaky pastry containing a mince meat and onion filling. Still wonderful, especially on a cold, rainy Scottish day.

**breeks**

## briquettes

A coal brick baked from coal dust or 'dross', and sold by coal merchants. Sometimes it was 'home-made' by filling old tins with wet dross and then letting them dry out and set. It was slow to light compared with coal and didn't provide the same degree of heat.

## bristle scrubbing-brush

This hard bristle brush was a bathroom item to enable you to get to the parts of your back you could not reach by hand.

## broken biscuits

'Any broken biscuits?' was a request made by children in grocers' shops. Sometimes biscuits which were broken could be obtained for a few pence.

## Broons

The much loved cartoon family from the *Sunday Post* who live at 10 Glebe Street. The family consist of Maw and Paw Broon, Granpaw Broon, Daphne Broon, Horace, Joe Broon, Maggie, Hen Broon, the Broon twins and 'the wee bairn'. Everybody has a favourite member of the Broon family. Men, of course, like the glamorous Maggie, while everybody has a soft spot for 'the wee bairn'.

## 'brothel creepers'

Suede shoes with thick crepe soles. Very popular in the fifties and sixties with 'teddy boys'.

## brown paper with pepper

This was heated and held against your cheek when you had toothache. The idea was that your mind was taken off the toothache because you were too busy sneezing!

*SQUEAK SQUEAK*

brothel creepers

## bubble gum

The popular pink gum which, after chewing, could be moulded by your tongue before you blew it into a bubble. Then it would burst with bits of it sticking to your face. Many a child got the belt for blowing it in class.

## bubbling

Having a wee bubble is to weep or cry. If you were forever crying you were called a bubbly-jock, the name given to a male turkey. I think we all had a wee bubble from time to time.

## bumbeleery cookie-bun!

Sometimes you were found out when kidding someone along so then you would quickly give the cheeky response, 'bumbeleery cookie-bun!' Bumbeleery is your backside.

## bumfle up

When your clothes were all crumpled, creased or wrinkled they were described as bumfled up. Then you might get a clout from your mother, especially if she had spent a long time ironing them.

## bundy clocks

Clocks used by tram drivers (motormen) to register their time and so keep their bosses happy. The tram would stop or slow down when they approached a bundy clock and out would jump the driver or conductress to check the time.

## bunkers for coal

Containers or spaces for coal, perhaps on a landing in a tenement, underneath a kitchen sink or against the back of a house. These were good places for 'hide and seek' but not appreciated by mothers when their offspring got dirty.

## bunnets

Most working-class men wore a bunnet, a soft flat-peaked hat. In fact many of them continued to wear it at home, especially if they were losing their hair.

## buroo

Where your father went when he was on the dole and looking for work. Derived from 'bureau', it was the forerunner of the Employment Exchange and Job Centre.

## buroo money

Unemployment benefit or dole money. Not much but it kept many a family going ... just.

## 'buses'

Perhaps you played at 'buses' on a flight of stairs which became the top deck of a bus. Someone would be the conductress and 'collect the fares', occasionally shouting, 'ding-ding' to indicate to the driver to start or stop the bus. The driver sat on the bottom step, turning an imaginary steering wheel and making engine noises.

## 'but and ben'

A traditional, rural, old-fashioned, two-roomed cottage. Often referred to in 'The Broons'.

## butter balls

Alternatively, it may have been margarine balls. These were dipped in sugar and were supposed to ease your sore throat.

## buttercups

You held a buttercup flower under your chin, and if the yellow colour was reflected on your skin, you liked butter. It appeared that everyone liked butter!

# C

## cadie

A leather hat worn by a boy. Some were styled after pilots' headgear with earflaps and a woollen lining. Great on a cold day.

## 'caller herring'

This was the shout of fish merchants coming around the streets with their horse and cart or barrow. 'Caller' meant fresh or newly caught and the herring was usually from Loch Fyne. The merchant had a set of scales on his cart and after purchase, he would wrap the fish in newspaper.

## candy apples

Apples with a stick through the core, dipped in sugar candy and allowed to set until solidified. Great, unless the apple was a bit 'sour' when you bit through the candy. This was a popular treat at fairs when they came to town.

## candy balls

Striped candy balls, the favourite for ruining young Scottish teeth.

## candy floss

Pure sugar melted into liquid, then run through small holes on a spinning head to form fine threads. It was then wrapped around a stick. Not as common as it once was but it used to be very popular in the past at various events and fairs. After eating one, you were left with a red, sticky mouth and chin. Something your dentist would not approve of.

### carbolic soap

The strange-smelling soap derived from coal tar that your mother used when she washed you in the bath. Afterwards you felt clean and fresh. The other favourite soap was Lifebuoy.

### carpet beater

This was a long-handled implement made of bamboo strips used to beat the dust and dirt out of carpets. The carpet would be hung over a washing line or fence, and then 'seven bells' knocked out of it. Occasionally it was also used by your father to administer some punishment.

### 'carry coal bags'

This term was used when you were being given a piggy-back on someone's bent back with your arms around their shoulders and neck. Also called a backie, cuddy-back or carry-code. It was also used when you played the game 'Knights on Horseback'. No wonder so many Scottish folks now have sore backs!

**carry coal-bags**

### castor oil

The common 'cure' for many an ailment, especially to ease constipation and as an emetic to induce vomiting. It has a very strong taste, and your mother probably held your nose as she administered it!

### cats' faces

Buns that looked like cats' faces. Very popular with children for that reason.

### cats' lick

The virtually non-existent wash you did when left to clean yourself. A wee dicht!

### caul

A weir or the head of a dam where you may have played. These were dangerous places, and much frowned on by parents and authorities if they found out you were there.

## cauld-kail-het-again

This was the name given to reheated soup of cabbage and vegetables. If there was a big pot it might be reheated every day with just some water added. The expression was also used when referring to a friendship that had been rekindled.

## causey

A pavement, road or street which was cobbled. Murder if you were going over them on your bike or bogie.

## causey-raker

The street-sweeper who came along with his barrow and brush. Could do with more of his sort nowadays!

## champit tatties

Simply boiled potatoes that had been mashed. Butter was then usually put on top. Wonderful!

## chanty

The chamber-pot that was usually found under the bed. Much used when the toilet was shared with other families or if it was some distance away, perhaps on a landing between flats.

## chappin' doors

... and running away! One of the things mischievous children got up to. See also 'ring bang skoosh'.

## cherry lips

Tiny hard jelly 'lips' sold in little bags. They were scented gum sweets and were popular with the girls.

## cheeny

Your mother or granny's best china. She would have murdered you if you broke any of it.

## chimney sweeps

When everyone had a lum the chimney sweeps were plentiful. They put their brush down the chimney having first blocked off the fireplace. Sometimes they got the wrong chimney and blackened someone else's home. If you could not afford a chimney sweep, you just stuffed paper up the lum and set it alight. If the Fire Brigade came out to a chimney fire that had been started deliberately, they fined you seven shillings and sixpence.

## chinese ropes

Coloured elastic bands looped together to make a long skipping 'rope'. One end was tied around your ankle and the other end to your friend's ankle. Then someone jumped in the middle through a series of sequences while you recited:

*Mister D, Mister I, Mister FFI.*
*Mister C, Mister U, Mister LTY*

## chips, on a bus run

Remember stopping the bus at a chippie when a bunch of you were out on a 'bus run' to allow everyone to buy chips? Those chips tasted fantastic!

## chittering-bites

The sandwiches or snack you were glad to eat when you came out of an unheated swimming pool, a loch or the sea, blue with the cold. It was supposed to stop you getting a chill by preventing your teeth chittering. Hypothermia had not been given a name in those days!

## Children's Hour

The much loved BBC Radio Scotland programme that ran up until 1964 with Kathleen Garscadden, originally known as Auntie Cyclone. We sat by the radio listening to every word.

## chipped fruit

If you asked a fruiterer for any chipped fruit, normally at the end of the day, he gave you the bruised and blemished fruit at a cut price. Well, you had to get your five portions a day somehow!

### christening piece

After a christening a small packet of cake or perhaps biscuit and jam, together with a silver coin, was given to the first person encountered of the opposite sex to the baby. It was a good idea to walk up and down outside a church when you knew a christening was taking place!

### chuckie

A hen or a chicken.

### chuckie-stane

A pebble or stone of the right dimensions for throwing, hopefully into the sea or loch, and not at anyone else. Named after the stone from the crop of a hen.

### chuntie-heid

A term given to someone deemed to be stupid or a slow learner.

### cigarette cards

When cigarette smoking was in its heyday, many of the brands had collection cards inside the packet. Mostly they were of famous footballers, squadron badges of the RAF, aircraft of the world, ships of the navy, flags of Europe, kinds of fish, film and radio stars, ships or cars. Small boys swapped them to make up sets or teams. Some children also inserted cigarette cards in the brake blocks of their bike, so that it sounded as though there was an engine as the card hit against the revolving spokes.

### cinnamon stick

This was used for eating or indeed smoking, when you hadn't quite reached the 'Woodbine stage'. Eating too much of it, or smoking all of the stick, had the same effect — it made you sick!

### claes line

The cord or rope line stretching between clothes poles which held up washing to dry. Wooden clothes' poles, sometimes called stretchers, with a notch in one end, were also used to ensure that the washing was high and would not trail on the ground. It gave the neighbours the opportunity to criticise the 'whiteness' of other neighbours' washings. It was an absolute disaster if the washing came off the line and had to be rewashed.

## clappy-doos

Large black mussels found on the seashore you may have collected in a bucket and taken home for eating. Not everyone's favourite, but a great name!

## cleaning the hoose

Before the days of fitted carpets and vacuum cleaners, mothers took great pride in having a 'clean hoose' and spent many hours cleaning, scrubbing and polishing, regardless of how humble it was. When the children came in from playing they were met with the same response, 'Now, watch where you put your feet, I've just cleaned that'.

## click

When you 'got a click' you had got yourself a friend of the opposite sex, probably to have a potential relationship with. Aye, that was the way it all started!

## clippies

The conductresses on busses and trams. Many of them were real 'characters' who dealt efficiently with any drunks, troublemakers, or individuals trying to evade purchasing a ticket. Formidable ladies they were!

clippie

## clocker

A broody hen that provided eggs in a family 'hen-run'. In days when food was scarce a few clockers were a wonderful bonus to the family larder.

## cloff

A wee nap during the afternoon, enjoyed by many a child. However if you overslept then your mother had trouble getting you to sleep at night.

## clootie dumplings

These were made as a treat at a birthday or at Christmas. They were large, dark fruitcake dumplings and contained mixing flour, spices, suet, currants and raisins. The mixture was kneaded into a dough and wee china dolls, buttons, thimbles, rings and silver thrupenny pieces were wrapped in greaseproof paper or bacofoil and placed in the mixture before being put in a 'cloot', a clean square of cotton, the four corners knotted up at the top. It was then placed in a large pot, half-filled with hot water, with a soup plate placed upside down in the bottom and cooked for a few hours. Ah, the smell when served hot! And, of course, you could always fry up the rest for breakfast.

## close-down on the telly

When broadcasting stopped every evening *God Save the Queen* was played followed by the 'spot' on your screen. Then you heard the voice saying, 'Remember to turn off your television'.

## close mouths

The close mouths of tenements. The close itself was a narrow area leading off the street to the passageway or stairs of the tenement. Used for congregating in and chatting to friends. The rear of the close was called the back close, usually a narrow musty passageway leading out to the rear of the tenement.

## cludgies

The name given to the famous toilets shared with your neighbours. These were overused and smelly and usually had cut-up newspaper instead of loo roll. Not recommended in the middle of a winter's night!

## clype

The person who was always a telltale, a snitch. Every class had one!

## coal fires

A wonderful warm focal point for any room, the 'open fire' gave out unsurpassed heat. The only problem was that the ash had to be removed in the morning when the new fire for the day was 'set or 'laid'. The open fire was also used to dispose of some small items of household waste such as potato peelings, tea leaves etc.

clype

## coalmen

A common sight on the streets. Coal merchants had to be strong and hard. After loading up their cart they would set off through the area shouting at the top of their voices to make their presence known. This type of communication was necessary so that the availability of coal would be heard by people in the attic flats of tenements. Orders were shouted down to the merchant who would then have to hoist hundredweight sacks of lumpy coal onto his shoulders, only protected by an empty coal-sack or leather covering, and carry them up the many flights of stairs. If your parents found pieces of stone or slate amongst the coal they would leave them aside and remonstrate with the coalman next time he came round.

## coal scuttles

The container for carrying coal into the house from the bunker or cellar. If the cellar was a long way off, or the bunker was outside, it was advisable that the coal scuttle was well-filled to last all night.

## cobbles

Many street surfaces were laid with smooth stones taken from river beds, or perhaps marble, and then 'cobbled' together. They were set in sand and bound with mortar. Cobblestone streets have gradually given way to asphalt though there are some still around.

## cock-a-leekie

Soup made with boiled chicken, leeks and finished with some prunes. Probably your 'posh' aunty made it.

## cock-a-breekie

Sometimes people of small stature were called this.

## cockie-breekie

This meant you were sitting astride someone's neck and shoulders. Sometimes called a 'high shoulder'. A bit scary if the person carrying you was very tall.

## cock or hen?

When boys joined in a game of football, the question was often asked of them, 'Cock or hen?' to determine the side they would play for. Usually such games had a 'million' players on either side, and you were lucky if you even got a kick of the ball!

## comb and paper

A comb with paper around it (usually that hard, horrible, tissue toilet paper) meant you could hum away with your own musical instrument.

## comics

Remember these? *The Hotspur, Eagle, Beezer, Tiger, Bunty, Judy, Girl's Crystal, Jackie, Diana, School Friend, Buster, Comet, Hornet, Knockout, Lion, Beano, Dandy, Topper, Magnet, Puck, Film Fun, Rover, Wizard, Victor*, etc. A lot of their stories were serials and you'd be desperate for the next issue to find out what happened next.

## conkers

Everybody remembers these! You took a fallen chestnut and put a hole through it from top to bottom with a heated pin (or you got a 'big person' to do it), then string was drawn through the hole and a knot tied on the end beneath the conker.

conkers

Next you challenged other children to a game, one holding out their conker by the top of the string while the other swung theirs to try and hit it. Children would carry a string of chestnuts around with them. To prepare the chestnuts for 'battle' some went to various lengths to harden them, perhaps baking or soaking the conkers in solutions. Each conker on the string was identified by its number of 'scalps'. If it had bust another fiver conkers then it would be a 'fiver'. Eight kills would make it an 'eighter' and so on. The government now wants to ban this game!

## coo's lick

A wayward tuft of hair at the hairline. When you became aware of it you were forever trying to flick it back.

coo's lick

## 'co orie in'

After being tucked up in bed, you were told to 'coorie in' or 'coorie doon'. This meant you were to snuggle or nestle down below the blankets and get warm and comfortable; wonderful and reassuring on a winter's night.

## corkers

A cotton reel with four wee nails driven in the top. Wool was wrapped around the nails and pulled over and around to make stitches. You could make teacosies and dolls' clothes using a corker. It was also sometimes called a 'knitting spool' or 'knitting nancy'.

## corner boys

During the Depression years of the 1920s, many unemployed men met at the corner of their street to while away the time. They could pass on rumours they had heard of potential jobs and talk football. Anyway, their wives were probably pleased to get them out of the house.

## corrie-fisted

Another name for left-handed people. Also called kippie, carhaundit or pally jeukit. In many educational establishments at the start of the 20th century, writing with your left hand was regrettably banned; indeed many pupils were punished if they tried to write using their left hand. It is derived from the Gaelic, *cearr*, meaning wrong hand.

## coronation parties

It was traditional at the time of coronations that street parties were held. Tables would be set out on the street and children would be served with jelly and pudding and given coronation mugs filled with sweets. At night bonfires were set alight. The last coronation was over 50 years ago, with the coming to the throne of Queen Elizabeth II in June 1953. There were similar parties held on the Jubilee of King George V.

## couthy

Plain or homely. Applies to various things including people who are sociable. You probably had an auntie who was 'couthy'.

## cosie

A warm, woollen scarf. Sometimes called a gravat. Your mother would wrap it around your neck and then the ends around your chest or pin them at the back with a safety pin. Knitting a scarf or cosie for Christmas or a birthday was common.

cosie

### coup

The rubbish dump or tip, or a filthy, untidy place you were told not to play on … or your room! 'This place is like a coup! Tidy it up.'

### crackle-stool

A three legged stool which usually sat near the fire. It was probably wooden and home-made. Because it was small you could get it in a good position to enjoy the warmth of the fire.

### cranachan

The lovely traditional Scottish dessert you may have eaten on special occasions. Made from whipped cream, honey, toasted oatmeal and raspberries. Terrific … if you liked whipped cream.

### crannie

Your wee finger, the pinkie. 'She's got him round her crannie'.

### craws' aipples

The crab apples that you thought would be wonderful but always gave you a sore stomach.

### craw-road

The most direct way between two places as in, 'as the crow flies'.

### creckle

When you had a sore, dry throat it was described as a 'creckle'.

### crew cut

crew cut

This was a style of haircut that was short all over (about a quarter of an inch) and tapered at the back and sides. 'Tony Curtis' haircuts, called after the famous Hollywood star, were also popular. 'Is that you got yersel' a Tony then?'

### crook

The fireplace chain with a hook that held the kettle over the fire. It could get very hot so you needed a cloth around your hand before you touched it.

### 'cruelty'

The 'cruelty' (a member of the RSPCC, the Royal Society for the Prevention of Cruelty to Children) was the person who looked after children who were reported as having been mistreated.

### crummock

A walking stick your grandfather would have had; some had fancy handles on them. 'When ah grow up grandpa, ah'm gonnae hae a crummock jist like yours.'

### crusts

Parents encouraged their children to eat the crusts of bread on the basis that it would give them curly hair! In reality it was to ensure that all food was used in a time of limited funds.

### cuddies

Donkeys or horses. 'Ye look as stiff and awkward as an auld cuddy.'

cuddy

### cullen skink

A thick fish soup made from smoked haddock, potatoes, onions and milk. Lovely, but not always enjoyed by children.

# D

### dainshoch

What you were called when you didn't like certain foods on your plate ... a fusspot. 'Right, if you won't eat it now you'll be having it for your tea!'

### daisy chains

You made these by joining up daisies, sometimes called gowans, to make a chain or necklace. It would be for yourself, your dollies or your dog or cat. Long fingernails were required to split the stem. Very frustrating when you put it around your neck and one part of the chain broke.

### daffin

Joking and carrying-on with your pals. You can no doubt think of some of the daft capers you got up to.

### dale

The diving board in your local swimming pool. It was called after a piece of wood used to measure corpses. Not a very reassuring thought as you dived off into the 'deep-end'.

dale

### darning

A fundamental skill especially at a time when socks were made with wool. Holes in the toe or heel were darned by bridging the hole in a criss-cross pattern with a darning needle and woolstring, hopefully of a similar colour to the sock.

### Davy Crockett hats

All the rage following the showing of the 1954 film, *Davy Crockett, King of the Wild Frontier*. It was a hat made of beaver skin with a tail attached. Very doubtful if the ones sold in Scotland were real beaver.

### deil's picter cairts

Literally, devil's picture cards. Better known as playing cards. Sometimes frowned upon in various traditional households.

### Dick Barton

Although not Scottish this radio series, broadcast between 1946 and 1951, was highly popular in Scotland. It was the BBC's first daily radio series and ran just after the evening news featuring Dick Barton, special agent and investigator, along with his pals, Jock Anderson and Snowey White.

### dictation books

The special school jotter used when the teacher dictated passages of narrative to test your ability to write and spell. If the teacher spoke too quickly you found yourself in trouble.

### digging for victory

The Ministry of Agriculture launched a slogan in 1939, 'Dig for Victory'. It encouraged people to transform their gardens into private allotments or rent a 'plot' somewhere to grow vegetables. Some allotments also had rabbits and chickens. Even a 'Dig for Victory' anthem was introduced.

*Dig! Dig! Dig! and your muscles will grow big,*
*Keep on pushing the spade.*
*Don't mind the worms*
*Just ignore their squirms*
*And when your back aches laugh with glee.*
*And keep on diggin'*
*Till we give our foes a wiggin'*
*Dig! Dig! Dig! to victory!*

## dinger

When you lost your temper, you were said to 'Go your dinger' or lose the place.

## dippen

The steps down to a river that your parents warned you to keep away from. Needless to say they were always an attraction especially to small boys.

## dizzy

To stand someone up on a date. Oh dear, your romantic notions and your confidence could be shattered when the agreed date didn't appear. Not nice, unless there was a valid reason of course.

## docken

The cure for being stung by a nettle by rubbing a docken leaf, from the dock plant, on the area of the sting. It is amazing that dockens always seem to grow beside nettles.

## dominie

The schoolmaster. Much feared and respected. We can all think of our favourite teachers and also the ones who were 'belt happy' or forever giving out punishment exercises.

## dook

When you had a swim, you 'went for a dook' in your swimming gear, probably a 'baithy' or 'dooker'. Swimming costumes were fine unless they were knitted!

## dooking for apples

Hanging over the back of a chair with a fork in your mouth, ready to spear an apple floating in the tub of water below. Or sticking your head directly into the water and grabbing an apple with your teeth. Not easy! Most folks just got their hair washed! It was a regular party game at Hallowe'en.

## doolander

A broad, flat cap. It gave you protection when the rain was belting down, and the wind threatened to drive it into your face.

## 'doon the watter'

Before the days of the package holiday abroad to the Spanish costas when a major source of enjoyment for many was a sail down the Clyde on a steamer.

## doorstane

The doorstep you sat on to play with your dollies or to read your comic or play at 'wee shops'. The trouble was your bottom got cold.

## doos

Pigeons. Pigeon fanciers are not quite as many as in the past when a lot of men had a pigeon loft and kept racing doos. A 'puddie-doo' was the name for a favourite or pet doo.

## doo's cleckin

The name used when your family consisted of only two children, a son and a daughter.

## dowt

The remainder of a discarded cigarette before the days of filter tips, sometimes also called a 'dowpie'. Could be relit with a pin through it, or the tobacco used to roll another cigarette or fill a pipe.

## drainpipe trousers

Extremely narrow trousers, usually with 14-in bottoms. Usually worn with a long, drape jacket.

## drappit eggs

Fried eggs in a pan. The smell was appetising, especially at breakfast.

## drawer

A metal shield placed over a large part of the aperture of a fireplace to suck or draw the air into a newly lit fire. Sometimes a newspaper was used to the same effect but this was always hazardous!

drainpipe
trousers

## dressing up

When wee girls put on their mother's peerie (high) heels, a stolen dash of lipstick and a long dress trailing behind them, they were 'dressing up'.

## drinking fountains

These usually had a metal cup attached with a chain and were popular before the days of hygiene regulations and vandalism. The cup would be pitted and dented from years of use but was very welcome on a hot summer's day. They were frequently found in parks or at street junctions. Sometimes there was a trough alongside for horses.

## drookit

You got drookit when you were drenched by rain. Especially when a sudden 'plump' fell.

## drooth

When you drank and still were dry after a long time playing outside, you probably said, 'I've a right drooth on me'.

## dulse

A kind of dried seaweed. It was sold in wee bags for a penny and was really quite tasty.

### dummy tit

The rubber teat for a baby; a comforter and a wonderful way to stop a baby crying, especially when dipped in sugar.

### dunny

Probably derived from the word 'dungeon'. The basement of a tenement containing the coal cellars and occasionally young lovers!

### dwam

What you were 'in' when daydreaming. A stupor. 'Sorry, pal. Could you repeat that. Ah wis away in a wee dwam.'

## eat up, yer at yer auntie's

When you were in someone's house and they were encouraging
you to eat more, they would say, 'Come on, eat up, yer at yer
auntie's!' Terrific, if there were plenty of cakes!

## eeksie-peeksie

When you shared out your sweets equally with your pals, you did
it 'eeksie-peeksie'.

## errant lo on

The errand boy who brought the order from the butcher or grocer,
probably on a bike with a metal basket at the front. If the orders
had been completed, he might even have given you a ride with
you sitting in the metal basket.

## eleven plus (the 'qualı')

The dreaded exam which determined your secondary education. It
was given to students in their last year in primary school. The
name derived from the age group of the students. The exam
consisted of an arithmetical test, a writing test, and a general
problem-solving paper.

## emulsion

The white, greasy substance in a large bottle sold by chemists to
supplement your food. The daily tablespoonful tasted of fish oil.

### 'face-or-a-blank'

A game played with cigarette cards. Your opponent held his cards concealed in his doubled fist. You guessed, 'Two a face', or 'Seven a blank'. If he held the cards face upwards in the first instance, he gave you two. If he had them the other way round, you paid up.

### 'fair' holidays

The traditional holiday period in the summer which varied depending on where you lived. Children of course, hoped for a holiday away, perhaps at the seaside, 'doon the watter'.

### fancy breid

Little cakes and biscuits. If your granny put down a plate of 'fancy breid' she would probably say, 'Take one'. The truth is you could have eaten the whole lot!

### fankle

When your bit of string/fishing line/wool was tangled up or twisted it was in a 'fankle'. Or when you got a wee bit confused someone might say, 'Don't get yursel' in a fankle!'

### farthings

A coin worth quarter of an old penny; farthing means 'fourth part'. There were 960 of them to the old pound! First minted in the 13th century and continued in use until the end of 1960.

### fernftickles

When your freckles were prominent
after playing out in the sun.
Worrying, especially if you were a
fair-skinned or red-headed girl.

### fever hospitals

Where individuals, mostly children, were isolated when they took
contagious diseases such as scarlet fever, diphtheria etc. In many
areas a red or red and white striped ambulance (fever van) took
them away. Parents could only come and wave to their children in
the ward through a small window.

### fidget

Perhaps you got punished at school for forever fidgeting, being
unable to stay still. The last thing you wanted was to share a bed
with a brother or sister who was forever fidgeting!

### finger church

Grandpa's finger church. He would say, 'Here's the church, here's
the steeple ... (while his fingers made arches and the roof) ... look
inside and see the people. Here's the minister walking upstairs ...
(all his fingers became steps with thumbs as legs) ... and here he
is saying his prayers'. Good old grandpa!

### fire

Setting a piece of paper on fire, by holding a glass or lens above it
to catch the sun's rays. It focused a 'miniature' sun onto the
surface of the paper, then it turned brown, smoked, and burst into
flames.

### first kiss

Where was it, and with whom?

first Sunday in May wearing your new outfit
Traditional day for wearing your new dress.

### five boys

Fry's milk chocolate bar with various faces of boys imprinted on
the chocolate. They depicted, desperation, pacification,
expectation, acclamation and realisation.

### florins

Introduced in 1847 and equal to one-tenth of a pound or two shillings. Remained in circulation until 1993 despite the introduction of the new decimal 10p piece in 1968. It was called a 'two bob bit'.

### fly cemeteries

Flat, baked, pastry cakes with a dense layer of cooked currants in the middle. Unfortunate name but delicious and filling.

### flypaper

Roll of sticky yellow paper hung from light fittings and ceilings to which flies stuck and then died; unsightly but effective. Usually found in food shops and kitchens.

### foggie-toddler

Bumble bees that annoyed you were called foggie-toddlers. Midges that annoyed were called something much worse.

foggie toddler

### footballs made with paper

When you and your pals didn't have a football old newspapers were wrapped up to form the shape of a ball, then tied with string. Fine until it started to rain!

### 'footering around'

Not doing much, or if a task was awkward it would be seen as 'an awfy footer'.

## Francie and Josie

Enjoyed by children and adults throughout Scotland; the much loved pairing of Jack Milroy and Rikki Fulton as the Glasgow 'wide boys'. 'Huullow-rerr chinas!' was their greeting. They first appeared in 1958 in a sketch in the Five Past Eight Show at the Alhambra in Glasgow. There was a joke that they 'murdered' for at least ten minutes in most shows, the 'Arbroath joke' and the audience were in stitches at this, even though they all had heard it many times before. The shortened version is as follows.

Francie & Josie

A salesman (Josie) comes to granny's door and knocks. Her grandson (Francie) answers it.
'Is yer granny in?' asks Josie.
'Naw, she's at Arbroath.'
'That's alright, I'll come back when she's finished.'

Their act together lasted for 38 years.

## french an

The toe cap on your boot that got very scuffed when you kicked stones and cans. Then you got cuffed for ruining your boots.

## frozen jubbly

A trianglular-shaped, frozen drink in a sealed, wax-paper wrapping which you sucked and sucked until the ice turned white and all the taste was out of it.

# gaberlunzie

A wandering beggar, tramp or sorner. They always knew which house would give them a bowl of soup and some coppers.

# galluses

Old fashioned braces for trousers, the type that required buttons on the back and front of your trousers.

galluses

# gamie

The gamekeeper in the park or estate who always chased you away. Some of them were cunning and actually caught you!

# gas mantles

The fragile, meshed mantle hoods used in gaslights and lamps. They were made either from guncotton or silk gauze or even rayon dipped in ammonium sulphide. When the gas ignited the gauze heated up, flouresced and radiated a brilliant, white light. But they were fragile and were forever being broken, particularly when the gas was being lit, or when being fitted on to the supporting bracket at the end of the swan-necked gas pipe that led up from the mantle-piece.

# gas masks

Gas masks were issued to everyone by the end of 1938. They were to help cope with gas attacks. Babies got a one-piece mask that covered their whole body. Children were issued with 'Mickey Mouse' gas masks designed with google eyes and a snout-like filter to resemble the famous cartoon character. There was a sensation of clammy breathlessness and a smell of rubber and disinfectant when the mask was donned.

## Geordie

The wonderful 1955 film starring Bill Travers from the book by David Walker. The tale is fondly remembered by many Scots. It's the story of wee Geordie, the under-sized lad who spends his savings on a mail-order physical development course to increase his height and improve his strength. In addition to the exercises he must also recite the 'Success Poem' every day.

*Today I may be small*
*But soon I will be tall,*
*I'll be strong,*
*I'll be long,*
*I'll grow the Henry Samson way,*
*Gaining a fraction every day.*
*Sound as a bell,*
*Feeling my muscles swell.*
*I'm the good old Scottish\* bull-dog breed,*
*And Samson will teach me to succeed.*

\*Changed from 'English' by Geordie!

Geordie eventually wins gold in the shot-put at the Olympic Games, and ultimately marries, Jean, his childhood sweetheart. Not a dry eye in the house!

## ginger

The popular name for a fizzy soft drink such as lemonade. If away on a picnic with your pals you would stick the bottle in a burn to cool it down.

## girds and cleets

A large circular ring or barrel hoop that was rolled along by hitting it with a metal rod called a cleet. Sometimes an old wheel off a bike was the gird and a stick used to keep it turning. Children would happily go from one end of a town to the other with their gird.
'Away an' see yer granny, son.'
'Ah cannae, maw. It's miles away an' ah've lost ma gird.'

### girny

When you were grumpy and irritable. (As
if you would be!)

### glaur

Mud and dirt. When you played outside
you ended up covered in this usually.
Nothing that soap and water didn't cure!

glaur

### glee-man

The name for the street entertainer who
played an instrument, probably a violin, for a few pennies.

### Glen Michael's Cavalcade

The TV show where Glen Michael,
supported by a puppet called
Paladin, showed cartoons requested
by viewers. It ran on STV.

### gloves-on-elastic

Gloves and mittens were attached to
a length of elastic that was fed
through sleeves to prevent their loss.
Sometimes you 'lost' a mitten up
your sleeve.

gloves on elastic

### gobstoppers

Multi-coloured sweets which changed colour as you sucked them.
Trouble was you had to take them out of your mouth to see the
latest colour, thereby making your hands sticky.

### golf

You perhaps started to golf using your father's, grandfather's or
uncle's old cleeks, jiggers, mashies, brassies and baffies, all with
hickory handles. Probably worth something nowadays.

### goonie

A child's nightgown, usually made of cotton or flannelette. What
Wee Willie Winkie was wearing when he ran through the town!

### 'going with'

When you had formed a romantic friendship with the opposite sex you were seen to be 'going with' them. 'Ah've been going with him now fur six months.'

### grace

Traditionally a grace was said before the family's main meal of the day. On many occasions it was Robert Burns' Selkirk Grace.

going with

*Some hae meat and cannot eat.*
*Some cannot eat that want it:*
*But we hae meat and we can eat,*
*Sae let the Lord be thankit.*

### grandpa's pipe

Many men, especially of the older generation, smoked pipes. They had a range of pipes, and probably a clay pipe or two as well. They generated quite a smelly fug inside a house. Perhaps you remember him shaking the dottle (left-over tobacco in the pipe) out and putting it in his baccy tin?

### granny can

The revolving chimney pot on a chimney head. 'See, there's an auld granny birlin' roon on the roof'.

### granny sooker

A large mint sweet much favoured by the older generation and given to children. It was often too strong for young tastes.

grandpa's pipe

### granny's bairn

A child, reared by a grandmother, who usually was regarded as a bit spoilt.

### greetin' match

When two children started to cry at the end of an argument it was called 'a greetin' match'. Also applied to adult fallouts that ended acrimoniously. 'Greetin' faced teenie' was the name given to a child or person who was forever complaining.

### Gregory's Girl

The 1981 film starring John Gordon Sinclair as a gangly, typical teenager, who loses his position in the school football team to the lovely Dorothy of 5A.

### guddle

If your bedroom was in a mess your mother would say it was in a 'right guddle', or perhaps a 'bourach'.

### guddling

Another name for tickling trout. You waded into the burn and by gently feeling for a brown, speckled trout with your arms deep in the water, you could catch it by gently stroking its underside before suddenly clutching it and throwing it onto the bank, all in one movement.

### guid words

Informal prayers said in a time of need or crisis, by someone who was respected.

### guineas

Coins with a face value of twenty-one old shillings (£1.05p). Sometimes, especially at auctions and horseracing, amounts are still quoted in guineas.

### guisers/galoshans

The older version of 'trick-or-treat', when you dressed up at Hallowe'en and went around neighbours, friends and relatives doing a party piece. In return you got fruit, sweets, and if you were lucky, money.

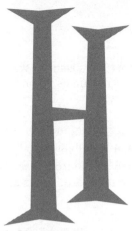

## half-crowns

Coins worth two shillings and sixpence in pre-decimal terms (12½p). These were in use until 1970.

## hamealdaemel

(Home will do me!) The popular phrase describing a holiday period spent at home.

## hand-me-downs

Remember these? Your big brother or sister's second-hand clothes. Sometimes they didn't quite fit and your mother had to make adjustments. If you were a boy with only older sisters you were in trouble.

hand-me downs

## havering

What you were accused of when you were thought to be talking nonsense.

## headers

Played by two boys with goals (probably jackets), a few yards apart. You threw the soccer ball into the air and headed it to try and score a goal. However if your opponent managed to head it back without it touching the ground, he got a point, and two points equalled a goal.

## heidies on the close wall

A favourite with many boys. Heading a rubber ball against a wall and seeing who could head it the most number of times. Mind you, the wall and your forehead got fairly dirty.

## 'heart fair roasted'

When your parents were worried or frustrated about you they may have said, 'You had ma heart fair roasted'. If the truth was told, every child caused their parents to have these sentiments at one time or another!

## hearth

The place where the fireplace was, and where the family would gather around on a cold winter's night. A metal or tiled fender ran around hearth, designed to contain any hot coals that fell out of the fire. This could happen when the fire was 'poked' to give it more air.

## heather-lowper

Someone from outwith your town. A visitor or a stranger. 'Ah don't know his face. He must be a heather-louper.'

## heebie-jeebies!

When something gave you a sense of fear or apprehension, you had these! Like going to school without your homework done!

## hide

The den or hide when you played 'hide and go seek', the game where you had to count to ten then go and find those who were hiding.

## hidey-hole

The place where you hid when you did not want to be discovered. Or it could be a wee 'hidey-hole' at home where you put some precious possessions.

### high doh

The state you got yourself into when you were excited or worried. Perhaps a visit to the dentist or anticipating presents from Santa on Christmas morning!

### highers

Studying and sitting your Highers could be a traumatic time. A Higher is the advanced exam taken under the direction of the Scottish Qualifications Authority, and is usually sat at the end of fifth year.

### hinmaist day

The final judgement day when you would be threatened with when you were naughty. 'Aye, you'll answer for this on hinmaist day, ma lad!'

### hippin

A baby's nappy. Unlike today, it was cloth and had to be washed and rewashed continually. Very eco-friendly!

high doh

### Hogmanay

The 31st December, a major date in the Scots' calendar. Traditionally everything had to be clean for the New Year. The old year would be let out through the window with a few minutes to go to midnight, then the New Year could come in at the door with the 'first foot'. Perhaps you stayed up late, fell asleep and missed 'the bells'. Perhaps your dad had one dram too many!

### hooley

A party which you went to which got a bit wild might be described as a 'hooley'. Your mother might say, 'No. You cannae go to Rauridh's party, it always ends up as a hooley'.

### hope kist

In the hope of a happy and fulfilling marriage, a girl would put away various items in a chest or the bottom drawer of a chest-of-drawers. Household goods such as dishes, pillow sheets, her mother's wedding dress, perhaps some jewellery, even baby clothing would be put away.

### horns

These were heard far and wide in shipyards, factories, Jute mills and the other industrial plants that dominated urban Scotland. It spelt the start of the day for working men and families alike. 'Hurry up! You'll be late for school. There goes the eight o'clock horn.'

### horse and cart

Horse-drawn carts and horse vans were once the popular method of transporting both goods and people. They were common until after the First World War. Roses have never been healthier!

### hot peas and vinegar

Very popular during and after the Second World War as peas were not rationed. Mostly sold in cafés where they came with plenty of salt, pepper and vinegar.

### hot water bottles

The stone ones were called 'pigs' due to their rotund shape. An alternative was bricks heated in the oven and wrapped in an old blanket.

### hotch-potch

Broth with pieces of mutton in it. Very filling and a great meal on a cold day.

### howdiewife

The midwife who delivered you if you were born at home.

### hudgie

Catching a hudgie was running after a moving vehicle and
holding on. Boys would run after slow-moving lorries and carts,
hanging on by their fingernails. If it was a horse and cart, and the
driver suspected that someone was catching a hudgie, he might
just flick his whip back to try and hit them.

### hula hoops

Plastic hoops which
you had to wiggle at
your waist to prevent
the hoop falling down.
Many a granny
thought she had
dislocated her hip after
'having a go'.

### hurdy-gurdy man

He turned a portable
organ called a hurdy-
gurdy that produced a
tune, while a pet
monkey went around
the assembled crowd
with a collection cup.

hula hoop

### huzzie

Sewing kit your mother had. Invaluable for fixing all darning and
sewing needs. Usually held a variety of colours of thread along
with various buttons.

## infare

Entertainment at home, perhaps with aunts and uncles joining in
the old Scotch songs. Many homes had pianos and someone was
sure to accompany the assembled group. Then a 'moothie' might
appear or a squeezebox, or someone might come away with a
joke or anecdote.

## ingle

Old-fashioned fireplace comprising the hearth, the fireside and the
mantelpiece. Tragically many were thrown out, and would have
been worth quite a bit of money nowadays.

## ingle-neuk

The corner beside the fire. A favourite spot for granny's chair as
she sat and read the *People's Friend*.

## inkwells

Most desks in school contained an
inkwell as the normal mode of writing
was with a pen nib. Unfortunately
some of them were also used as
receptacles for chewing gum!

## ink monitors

The schoolchildren allocated the job
of ensuring the inkwells were kept
topped up. You were guaranteed to
have blue hands by the end of the
day.

ink monitor

## iron lungs

Patients were placed in these contraptions when their central nervous system was impacted through illnesses such as polio, and they required assistance to breath.

## itchy coo os

Rose hip seeds you put down your friends' backs as a joke because they caused itching.

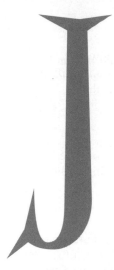

## Jackets for goalposts

The tradition was for jackets to be put down on the ground to indicate goalposts for impromptu games of football. Led to many a heated discussion as to whether the ball had 'hit the post' or not. Sometimes the 'goal' was between a lamppost and a wall, which saved any debate.

## Jags

Commonly used name for injections applied by hypodermic syringes. The doctor and nurse came to the school, and you all duly lined up, trying hard to be brave.

## Jannie

The man who really ran your school. It was heavy work when the jannie had to keep the furnace topped up with coal during the winter, or ensure that the fires in each classroom did not go out. In some schools he also noted the attendance on the slate that hung behind each classroom door.

## Jawbox

Old fashioned sinks, mostly black, and usually boxed-in with a small cupboard or bunker underneath. They were used to wash the dishes, and where each member of the family also washed each day.

### jeely jaurs

Jam jars used for containing brambles or tadpoles (powarts), or even as 'currency' to get you into the cinema. It was a tragedy if you fell and broke a jar on your way to the 'pictures' then couldn't get in.

### jeely pieces

Sandwiches wrapped in paper and traditionally flung out the window by your mother, so that you could keep playing without having to come in.

### jenny-a-things

The local shop you went to for messages. It sold a wide range of types of goods with open containers of a variety of foodstuffs, including coffee. The aroma in the shop could be most appetising.

### jenny langlegs

Large craneflies (daddy longlegs). Fragile flies that always seem to find their way into the house in the summer.

### jew's harp

The small musical instrument which is held against the mouth or lips and plucked with the fingers. Still around, but particularly popular in the early years of the 20th century.

jenny langlegs

### jouk up a close

Hiding in a tenement closemouth, or upstairs on a landing while playing a game. If a housewife was washing the stairs you might find yourself getting a bawling out.

### juke boxes

They were all the rage in the local cafés playing the latest hits on a Shellac 78-rpm record juke box, or a Seeburg Corporation 45-rpm vinyl record juke box. For a small amount of money you could select the records of your choice.

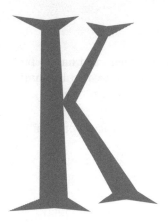

# kazoo

A simple musical instrument which, when hummed into, gave a buzzing sound. Some schools had an 'orchestra' totally composed of kazoos. You got a similar sound when you wrapped toilet tissue over a comb, put it to your lips and blew over it!

# keeker

When you got a black eye it was said to be a keeker. The trouble was everyone wanted to enquire how you got it. The standard answer was, 'Aye, but you should see the other fella!'

# keepie-uppie

Playing with a 'tanner' (sixpenny) ball, heading, kneeing or kicking it while not allowing it to touch the ground. Some children, boys and girls, had a natural ability and could achieve quite high scores.

# keys

Thumbs up and a cry of 'keys' or sometimes 'barley' indicated a truce in a game. It meant a suspension of the rules until a dispute was resolved. They should try it in the Scottish Parliament.

# key on a string behind the door

The key that was hung on a piece of string behind the front door of a house, which you pulled through the letter box to let yourself in.

### kick-the-can

The game where an old can was placed in a 'den', and had to be guarded against the other team kicking it out of the den. Bedlam!

### 'kiltie kiltie cauld bum'

Shouted by naughty children at men wearing Highland dress and assumed to be 'true Scotsmen'.

### kindling the fire

The morning ritual in most homes. Clearing away the ash from the fire of the night before and putting small sticks (kindling) onto a bed of twisted newspaper.

### kitchen ranges

The range of ovens and hobs fired by coal. The forerunner of the cooker.

### 'kkt'

Kiss, kick or torture! The game where the boys ran after the girls and when they caught them gave them this option! Needless to say most opted for a kiss!

### knickers tucked in

Summer days at the beach, the girls paddling with their dress tucked into their knickers. Ah, the good old days.

### knife sharpener/grinder

The person who came around and sharpened knives on his grindstone for a few pence.

## knee-hicht

A small child who barely comes up to your knee would be described like this. 'Get that food intae you or you'll forever be knee-hicht'.

## knock-back

A refusal by a lady when asked to dance by a gentleman.
'Ur ye dancing?'
'Naw, it's jist the way ah'm staunin'!'

## laldie

When you were encouraged to 'gie it laldie' it meant getting stuck in, being robust, doing it with vigour and gusto … you get the picture. Usually to be heard from the sidelines at a football game.

## larachs

The ruins of old houses where you played. You had to be careful because a lot of the old stones could be slippery with moss.

## last

The metal frame in the form of a shoe on which your father mended the family shoes. He would patiently take off the old soles, then stick a new one on, and then with his mouth full of tacks he would hammer each around the outside of the sole. If his standard of work wasn't too good you knew all about it next day!

## last day of school term

You were allowed to bring games into school on the last day of term. The teachers encouraged board games which were seen as educational.

## last to take a 'bought cake' if there were visitors

If your parents had visitors you were instructed, under pain of death, not to take a cake from the plate until the guests had had their choice.

## latrine

A toilet, sometimes just a hole in the ground, with a floor plate. Remember the pong?

### laughing policeman

By putting a penny in this amusement machine the figure dressed as a policeman would laugh heartily, 'Ho, Ho Ho!'

### lavvy chains

When high cisterns were located on the wall behind the loo to give a good flush of water, the pulling 'chain' could be string, rope or indeed chain. Sometimes they would have an ornate china handle.

### leerie

The person, male or female, who came round with a cleek to light the communal gas lights each evening. They had to be careful not to damage the mantles.

### lemonade bottles

At one time used as 'currency' or, on taking them empty back to the shop, you could usually get a thruppenny piece for each bottle returned.

### letters up the lum

Mostly sent to Santa at Christmas, detailing a list of toys and stating that the individual had been good all year long. If your father read it before it floated up the chimney, he would comment, 'Aye, an' you'll be lucky!'

### liberty bodices

Worn over your vest to keep you warm. A close-fitting, fleecy garment for girls.

### licking the bowl after baking

Many a child hung around waiting for the baking mixture to be used, so that they could spoon out or lick what remained in the bowl. Clootie dumpling mixture was particularly tasty!

### Liquafruta cough cure syrup

An old-fashioned expectorant that produced mucus. The taste either killed you or cured you.

### links

Sausagemeat encased in skins, still 'linked'. Not square-sliced Lorne sausage meat.

### linoleum

Not so popular now but used to be manufactured in Kirkcaldy, giving the town an interesting aroma. It was made from cork and linseed oil, then waxed. It could be scrubbed and polished, usually with Cardinal floor polish.

### liquorice stick

There were two types. Either a root of liquorice for chewing, or a penny liquorice stick.

### Loch Ness monster

Flicking a rope to make ripples go snaking right to its end.

### Lord's Prayer

Everyone had to stand in class, close their eyes, and recite the Lord's Prayer at the start of each school day.

### loupin the cuddie

Playing leapfrog in the playground. Sometimes it involved quite a number of children who, when they had been 'louped over', ran to the front to be 'louped over' again.

### lovehearts

Fizzy fruit sweets in various flavours, with a love message on one side. 'Kiss me', 'I want U', 'My wee girl', Dream girl'. You may have slipped one in class to the girl or boy you fancied.

### lucky-bags

A lucky bag could be purchased for thruppence and would contain sweets and novelties. The contents varied, so it was just your luck what you got. The term was used in other ways. 'Ah think they must have got that wean in a lucky bag!'

### 'lucky' middens

In tenement property the midden usually consisted of a brick lean-to attached to the wash-house. Inside would be up to four galvanized bins where tenants put their rubbish. A 'lucky midden' was one where you would allegedly find wonderful treasures thrown out by a better-off tenant. Children who did this were said to be 'proging the middens'. The bins were emptied by 'midden-men', sometimes called scaffies, who shovelled the middens' contents into large baskets and carried them to the refuge/bin/'clenny' lorry. Many had their trousers tied below the legs to prevent rats and mice running up their legs.

## lucky potatoes

A piece of confectionery covered in cinnamon with a trinket inside. Delicious, but you had to get the trinket out first before you sunk your teeth into it.

## luggie

The small bucket or container you tied around your waist when berry picking. It had a handle or 'lug' projecting from the side. If you didn't have a luggie you got yourself a large tin.

## lumber

'Getting a lumber', usually at the dancing, was managing to befriend someone of the opposite sex. For many people that was the object of going to the dancing!

## luss

The dreaded dandruff! Sometimes difficult to get rid of as medicated shampoos were not around then.

## Macallum

Two scoops of vanilla ice cream with a dash of raspberry served in a dish. Nearly as good as a knickerbocker glory!

## magic lanterns

The forerunners of projectors, normally used in village and church halls for community slideshows. Sometimes it was a very basic machine with a fuzzy opaque picture projected onto a white sheet.

Magic Lantern

### mangle

A large roller wringer usually in a wash-house or steamie. The rollers could be eight inches or ten inches in diameter. Mostly used for squeezing the water out of bulky items like blankets. A large handle at the top adjusted the pressure of the rollers. You had to watch your fingers!

### marbles

Decorative glass balls of varying size. The colour and size determined the 'value' of the marble in terms of how many times one had to hit it before the marble was won.

### maskin-pot

The teapot. To mask the tea was to brew it.
'Ah told ye tae brew this tea, no' stew it!' or 'This isnae tea, it's hot watter knocked stupid!'

### McFlannels

First broadcast in March 1939, the McFlannels was a radio serial based on a working-class Glasgow family. It was written by Helen W Pride and was compulsive listening on a Saturday night with a variety of characters including Old Granny McFlannel … 'Oh my me ma maw, ah'm no wantin' tae be a burden tae ye'. The show also had the posh Mrs McCotton plus the late Molly Weir as 'Poison Ivy'.

### mealie pudding

A white pudding made with a little meat and oatmeal. The taste and smell when it was frying was wonderful.

### means testing

In times of depression various criteria were rigorously applied before someone could receive any benefit. In some cases an inspector would enter a household and check what the family were eating.

## menage

A thrift system with payments through a neighbourhood collector. When your 'menage book' got to an agreed credit limit you could go to a specific warehouse and choose items up to that value. Many families were dependent on this way of purchasing.

## mental arithmetic

The arithmetical tests given orally by your teacher which really sharpened up your ability with numbers ... or threw you into a panic!

## messages

Going for the groceries or running an errand for a neighbour. Sometimes you might be rewarded with a penny.

## metal strip machines

Found in railway stations and piers. They were small machines where, for a few pence, you could spell out a name or message on a metal strip. Girls often had bangles with their name on it. Forerunner of Dymo tape.

## milk bottles

Now a rarity, but delivery of milk in bottles via the milkmen each day was common up until the 1990's. Before milk bottles, milk was brought around in the milk 'cairt' and you went out to fill up a chipped blue enamel container, or similar, from the tank.

## milk monitors

Selected children were allowed into school early each morning to help fetch the crates of milk bottles to each class. The bottles contained a third of a pint. Milk monitors usually received an extra bottle if there were any spare bottles left.

## mince n' tatties

An old-fashioned but still loved dish of steak mince, boiled potatoes with perhaps a bit of onion. The ultimate meal!

## mindin'

A wee mindin' was a present, perhaps from a grandparent or auntie, offered as a memento.

## minnows in a jar

Remember fishing with jam jars to catch minnows in a local loch? Half-filling your jar with water to give it weight, adding a piece of bread and casting your jar, tied by string into the water. Then, when you got home, having to put them down the toilet under pain of death by your parents!

## mission halls

Mission halls were popular, independent, small churches. Children liked the Bible quizzes and the sweets handed out.

## moonlight flittings

These occurred when a tenant with significant rent arrears packed all their goods and chattels and disappeared during the night.

## mort-heid

A turnip hollowed out into the shape of a head at Halloween. A candle would be placed inside, and it would be carried around in the dark either on a string or at the top of a stick. It was said to represent death.

## multiplication tables

Chanted each day in primary schools until you could recite them in your sleep. In later life you appreciated their value.

## mump the cuddie

The game in which you and your pals all sat on your hands, then 'raced' each other to a winning line. Could be sore on your hands.

### napery press

The linen cupboard where your mother carefully put her ironed sheets, etc.

### National Health specs

Spindly, wire spectacles much detested by children, especially girls. Then you were probably called 'specky' at school.

### National Health teeth

Wallies! Supplied to a generation who had failed to look after their teeth. It was before fluoride was applied to water supplies. Normally left to soak overnight in a glass.

### navy gym knickers

Standard wear for girls during school gym: heavy, cotton, navy knickers. Gave the boys something to snigger about!

### Ne'erday

New Year's day, when you were probably very sleepy if allowed to stay up late on Hogmanay.

### nevelling

A fistfight in the playground. A large group of boys urging on the two contestants in the middle. A teacher usually intervened and the two boys probably got the strap or other punishment for their troubles.

## newspaper as toilet paper

Cut up squares of newspaper were used before toilet paper became available, and affordable, by the general population. Sometimes people used the tissue paper that had been wrapped around fruit.

## newsreels

The Pathé Pictorial and Movietone News in the cinema. Very important during war years when it was necessary to encourage morale at home. It was always slightly out of date.

## nicky-tams

Ties below the knee for workers' trousers. Usually made of leather or string. Wearers included farm workers and midden-men (dustbin men).

## nit nurse

Checked children at school for head lice and vermin. A fine comb was dragged through hair to establish their existence. Parents were 'black-affronted' when a child reported that the nurse had found lice. 'They must have come from that wee Graham you sit beside!'

## nylon stockings

Became particularly popular during the Second World War when American servicemen brought them over for girlfriends. They had seams up the back and were prone to laddering. Nail varnish was used to stop the ladder 'running'.

## oil-cloth table covers

Popular as they were 'hard wearing' and easy to clean with a damp cloth.

## 'old-fashioned'

A child called this was seen as a bit advanced for their age or even somewhat precocious. 'Ah think she's an old-fashioned bit o' stuff who's been here afore.'

## old men's huts

Provided by some councils for older men to go and pass the time playing draughts, dominoes or reading newspapers.

## onion men

Mostly Frenchmen or Bretons generally, known as 'Onion Johnnies', dressed in a striped shirt and beret, selling onions tied in strings to their bicycles.

## O or Wullie

Oor Wullie (proper name, William Russell), first appeared in the *Sunday Post* in March 1936. A host of wonderful characters appeared with Wullie in his various adventures including, Fat Boab, Maw and PC Murdoch. Wullie was and is forever age nine, wears only dungarees, and at some stage in each story sits on his pail. 'Jings, crivvens, help ma boab!'

### 'oot fur a hing'

Before the days of television when a woman, man or child, would open their window, mostly in tenements, place a cushion on the windowsill, and watch the comings and goings in the street.

### open-air religious meetings

Held at street corners. Usually one of the party had a musical instrument to accompany the singing. Neighbours' windows would be opened so they could listen.

### orange juice

Bottles of condensed orange juice were distributed during and after the Second World War for all children.

### outings on 'Fair' Saturdays

The traditional 'fair', the trade holidays, fell at various times for different towns during the summer. Some people were unable to 'get away', especially in times when no holiday pay was given to employees, and so an outing on only one day became, in effect, their holiday.

### outsider

These were the first or last slices of a loaf of bread; usually much thicker than the other slices and much sought after by hungry family members.

### oxter

Your armpit that your mother told you to wash each day.

## pace egg

An Easter egg. Either hard-boiled or made of chocolate. If hard boiled, someone would draw a face on it.

## packman

The salesman who regularly came around the doors with his case full of household items, such as brushes and cleaning materials.

## palaver

Idle chat. Some people were notorious for coming 'away with' a lot of palaver.

## palliasses

Before spring mattresses, many pillows and mattresses were filled with straw. Made life difficult if you were prone to sneezing.

## panel

Panel of doctors' patients. You were said to be 'on the panel' of doctor such-and-such.

## pan

Common name for your head or skull. 'If you don't behave I'll knock your pan in!'

## palmy

A slap on the hand by another hand, usually the teacher's. Probably in the first few years of primary school.

## pandy

A stroke on the hand with the tawse. You were lucky if you only got one!

## papsy

A game whereby pennies, ha'pennies and the cardboard tops off milk bottles, were 'papped' (thrown) at the base of a wall. Nearest to the wall won and took the other items that had been 'papped'.

## parachute silk dresses

Dresses made out of the silk used for making wartime parachutes. A good example of recycling.

## Para Handy

The wonderful books and TV series about a crafty Gaelic skipper of a Clyde puffer, the *Vital Spark*. The skipper, Para Handy, is the nickname of the fictional character Peter MacFarlane. The stories mostly focus on his pride in his puffer, 'the smertest boat in the trade', and the high jinks he and the crew get up to during their voyages. The other members of the crew are all characters in their own right, Macphail, the engineer, Dougie the ship's mate and Sunny Jim, the young deckhand. There were three television adaptations of the stories, the first with Duncan Macrae as Para Handy, then Roddy McMillan as the skipper, and finally Gregor Fisher in the starring role.

## parish

On the parish. If someone did not have sufficient stamps on their employment card or had run out of 'benefit' through long unemployment, they went 'on the parish', or public assistance to get food, clothing and coal.

## parritch-time

Breakfast, usually of porridge. 'Come on, get up. It's parritch-time and it's getting' cauld!'

## pavement cracks

Game where children tried to walk or run without putting their feet on the wee gaps between pavement stones.

## pawkies

Wee woollen mittens, probably knitted by your mother or granny. A favourite gift at birthdays.

## pawn shops

Used much in the past. The three golden balls hanging outside the shop were a familiar sight. They originated from the House of Lombard who operated pawn shops throughout Europe. The windows of pawn shops displayed unredeemed pledges for sale. Blankets, bed-linen, dinner sets, cutlery, wedding rings and watches were popular items to pawn. When you misbehaved you might have been threatened with, 'If you don't behave I'll pawn ye and sell the ticket!'

## pea shooters

Small plastic or wooden tubes which you blew into to fire peas. Thankfully no longer popular.

## pea-soupers

Thick fog caused by coal fires, heavy industry and lack of wind. They were common in winter. Coming home late from school in one of these could prove difficult, with buses and cars crawling along and difficult to see. You probably put your scarf over your mouth and were very relieved to reach home.

## 'pee-the-beds'

The name you gave to dandelions. Once most of the petals were off you blew the remaining seeds to tell the time! The name was given due to the property of the plant which acted as a diuretic.

## peenies

Usually 'wrap around' peenies, an apron worn by many women. Some women seemed to wear peenies and curlers all day!

## peelie-wally

What your mother said to you when you were looking ill. 'You're gey peely-wally'. If you didn't feel ill before, that certainly made you feel sick!

peelie-wally

It means excessively pale and off-colour. Maybe a bit 'hingy' also, that is hanging about the house not quite yourself.

## peepy-show

The cinema or 'pictur hoose'. Sometimes naughty children went in a group, one paid to get in then opened the exit door to let their pals in. If the cinema was divided up into various categories of seats, such as the sixpenny rows, the shilling rows and the one-and-sixpenny rows, it was not unusual to see people changing seats during the performance!

## peerie

A spinning top spun with the aid of a small leather whip. Sometimes children painted them so that they became more interesting as they spun. Probably comes from the Scots word for pear as that was the rough shape of the top.

## peerie heels

Your mother's high-heeled shoes that you tried on as a girl. 'Hey, have you been trying on my shoes?'

## pencil line on the back of girls' legs

To give the impression that stockings with a seam were being worn. Sometimes it was in Biro. You really needed someone else to draw it on for you.

## penny caramels

Plus penny whoppers, penny dainties and Highland Toffee, usually in the 'penny tray' at the tuck shop near a school. Kept the dentist busy!

## permanent waves

Ladies' perms which were popular in the middle of the 20th century. It involved the curling of naturally straight hair by applying waving lotion once the hair had been set in rollers.

## petted lip

The sulky look with your lower lip stuck out when you were in the huff. 'Don't give me that petted lip!'

petted lip

## pey bree

Soup mostly made with peas. It could get gey windy later.

## phone boxes

Red phone boxes which stood on street corners or on the main road through a village. In the original boxes you had to insert tuppence in the slot before dialling. When you heard the other person's voice you pressed button 'A'. Button 'B' got you your money back if your call did not get through.

## picking brambles and berries

The traditional time each autumn when families got empty tins with string on them, put the string 'handle' around their necks and picked brambles for jam making.

## pieces and jam

The traditional jeely sandwich, made out of a plain loaf. Fed many a starving wean.

## pig's feet

Boiled pigs' feet was a tasty meal, provided you kept your eyes shut!

## pink paraffin man

The man who came around in his van and provided paraffin, mostly for heating. There was always a smell of paraffin off him.

## pin leg

An artificial leg made of wood. Many were made after the First World War.

pig's feet

### pipe cleaning stairs

Cleaning of stairs, notably in tenements, when tenants took their weekly turn, using a cake of white pipeclay. Once cleaned, old newspapers were put down on each step to protect them until they dried.

### 'pit on'

The insincere face you were sometimes accused of putting on.

### playpieces

The sandwich you took to school to eat at playtime, just after your free bottle of milk.

### playing in puddles

One of the joys of a Scottish childhood was playing in puddles, splashing, jumping and getting generally soaked.

### plasticine

Man-made malleable, dough-like substance with a pungent smell, much loved by children at school and at play. Used for making models of wee dogs, giraffes, or just rolling into balls.

### playing at wee shops

Girls made 'wee shops' using bricks as a counter, and picking weeds to provide 'goods' to sell. Perhaps docken leaves for fish, grass for chips and coloured glass for money.

### plooks

When you found a plook, pimple or blackhead on your face it was a disaster. 'Ah cannae go tae school, ah've goat a big plook oan ma chin!'

### plunk

To plunk school was to play truant. You might then be called a 'fuggie'. See 'school attendance officers'.

## pogo stick

A jumping stick with handles and pegs
for your feet. There was a spring-loaded
base so that you could hop along.

## poke

This could mean a poke of ice cream (cone), a paper bag, or it
could be a poke in the eye, a pokey hat, or 'in the pokey',
meaning jail when the police had someone in the 'bag'.

## police boxes

A blue box with an orange light on top, activated when the police
station wanted to contact the policeman on the beat. They were
located at various key points throughout towns and cities. Dr
Who's Tardis is one of them.

## Pontefract cakes

Liquorice sweets about the size of an old penny. Very tasty.

## porridge in a drawer

A week's supply of porridge could be stored in a drawer by letting it cool and set. Once solidified it was cut into slabs for future meals.

## 'potatoes laughing at you'

Unpeeled potatoes which had burst their skins in the cooking pot were said to be 'laughing' at you.

## potted held

An old-fashioned 'delicacy' produced by boiling the head of a sheep and then taking the mush that was produced from it and setting this in gelatine. It was served cold and you were better eating it without knowing the contents.

## potter's wheel

Intermission scene on early BBC TV programmes in the early days of television, when there was a gap between programmes.

## postman's knock

The game where you shouted out the number of a person of the opposite sex, and then gave them a kiss. Sometimes it was more than 'just a wee cheeper'!

## powarts

Tadpoles in a jar.

## pow

Your head or 'napper'. Someone would say, 'Blessings on your curly pow'.

## powdered milk

During and after the Second World War, tins of powdered milk were issued to all families with small children.

## prefabs

Prefabricated metal-clad bungalows designed to quickly alleviate the post-war housing shortage. Some were still standing at the end of the last century.

## press

The family cupboard where various items were stored.

## puddock

The frogs or toads you
found. 'Don't you dare
bring that puddock
into this house!'

## puggy

If you went out with your pals perhaps you all put money in the
communal puggy or kitty.

## pulley

The popular hanging clotheshorse of long parallel bars pulled up
by a pulley rope. Normally suspended from the ceiling of a
kitchen, or a bathroom, if you had one.

## 'quilts with sleeves'

On very cold nights, coats were flung on the top of beds to provide added warmth in the days before central heating. Sometimes known as 'poor man's eiderdowns'.

### Radio Caroline

Pirate pop radio station ship moored outside territorial waters.
The former ex-ferry *Fredericia* was converted to MV *Caroline* with
radio studios built on the upper decks behind the ship's bridge. A
tall aerial tower was installed near the bow. On Good Friday 1964,
Simon Dee the DJ announced:
'This is Radio Caroline on 199, your all day music station.'

### Radio Luxembourg

Used to be found on the
208 metre wavelength on
the radio. A favourite for
early pop and Top Twenty
programmes and it
launched many a career,
such as Jimmy Saville.
Now no longer
broadcasting in English.

Radio Luxembourg

### rag store

Store where mostly old
woollen goods were
exchanged for a small
amount of money.

### ragabuss

A person who was poorly dressed, perhaps in rags. Some kindly
people would pass on old clothes which were better than the ones
worn by the individual.

### railway waiting rooms with coal fires

Warm, smelly and draughty places where you could wait on a cold winter's day for your train.

### rain mates

For keeping your head dry. A folding, plastic headcover.

### ran-dan

Out on the ran-dan was to be looking for a good time or wild spree, usually with members of the opposite sex.

### ranges

Fireplace ranges, usually manufactured by Carron, comprised an oven, a cooker, and a large iron arm with a hook at the end which could swing out over the fire. A lot of the cooking pots and kettles had metal handles on the top that allowed them to be suspended by the hook. It was black-leaded with the 'steel' bits rubbed with emery paper.

### ration books

At the start of the Second World War each family was issued with ration books which detailed their entitlement to food and other goods. Households had to register with their local shops, and were allowed to use their points only in these shops. In this way, each shop was provided with enough goods to meet the demands of their registered customers.

Each person was allowed 16 points per month to use on whatever food items they wished from the stocks available. The number of points was later raised to 20 per month. Some items, such as fish, potatoes and peas, were never rationed, although fish was occasionally in short supply. Children under five were allowed a half-ration of meat, and children between five and 16 held a separate blue ration book that entitled them to fruit and other health-promoting products. Additional rations were given to pregnant mothers. A typical adult weekly ration was: butter 50g (2oz), bacon 100g (4oz), sugar 225g (8oz), meat to the

value of one shilling and sixpence, three pints of milk (1.8 litres) but sometimes only two pints, cheese 2oz (50g) and tea 50g (2oz). A jar of jam 450g (1lb) was allowed every two months. Dried eggs were rationed to one packet every four weeks and sweets to 350g (12oz) every four weeks. It wasn't only food that was rationed; furniture, curtain material, clothes and blankets, too, had to be bought with dockets issued by the government.

### reception on your transistor radio

Standing next to an electric street lamp gave you better reception.

### relievers

A game requiring two teams and a 'den'. One team had to catch the other and take them to the 'den'. However a member of the team who was not in the den could 'relieve' those in the den by touching them and shouting, 'relievers!'

### rhone pipe

The drainpipe, usually made of cast iron, running from the gutters of a building down to the ground. Sometimes you shinned up them!

### rhubarb and sugar

A stick of rhubarb accompanied by a poke of sugar to dip the rhubarb in.

### rickets

Unfortunately a common problem with many Scottish children in earlier days last century. It was caused by a lack of vitamin D, mostly through lack of exposure to sunlight. It produced a softening of the bones so that some people had 'bowly legs'.

### rickle o' bones

When your parents thought you were too thin, they would tell you to eat-up as you were a 'rickle o' bones'.

### ring bang skoosh

Naughty game played by children when they rung a neighbour's bell and ran away.

### roarin' gemme

Curling on a local loch when the ice was thick enough. It was called 'roarin' due to the noise the stones made when travelling over the uneven surface of the ice.

### roly-polies

Rolling sideways down a grass hill. Your clothes would get dirty, and if the grass had been recently cut then you ended up covered in cuttings.

### room and kitchen

A flat that was one room better then a 'single end'. Families in tenements tried to move on from 'single ends' to the more commodious room and kitchen. Your mother would state, 'Ah've got ma name in for a 'room and kitchen'.'

### rush-fever

The dreaded scarlet fever. See 'fever hospitals'.

# S

### sade

Peat or sods for burning. They would be piled up in an outbuilding to keep them dry.

### sandshoes

'Sannies', plimsolls or gutties were the basic forerunners of today's trainers.

### school attendance officers

Responsible for chasing up truants (plunkers) from school. Would get the names from the school then visit each house.

### school cruises

At one time, mostly in the 60's and 70's, 'educational cruises' to various countries including Spain and Portugal, North Africa and Scandinavia, were popular. Lectures were given each day on the places to be visited. Ships such as the *Dunera*, *Devonia*, and *Nevasa* were used.

### school dances

Girls lined up on one side of the gym and the boys on the other. The memory brings you out in a cold sweat!

### school dentist

The dreaded school dentist with his antiquated foot-operated drill and limited equipment.

school dentist

## school report cards

Some school report cards were issued every six months, and had
to be initialled by a parent. Against each subject was a rating: E
for excellent; VG + very good plus; VG very good; VG- very good
minus; G good; FG fairly good; U unsatisfactory (though some
cruel children maintained it stood for useless!)

## school writing books

To help you move onto 'real', 'joined-up' writing, a pre-printed
jotter was provided where you had to copy the letters using a
'thin-up' stroke and a 'thick' downward stroke of your pen. If you
were particularly poor at writing the teacher might say, 'Looks
like a hen washed its feet in your inkwell and walked over that
page'.

## scliffing

When you dragged your feet when walking and were reprehended
by your parents. 'If you get a hole in they shoes you'll be in
trouble!'

### scoot

The nimbleness of young people. Do you remember scooting aboot all over the place and never getting tired?

### Scotch-horses

Game where you linked arms across your back with another boy or girl, while a third person acted as a driver.

### scouts

Clasping your hands for someone to put their foot in the clasped fingers, and so be helped over an obstacle like a fence, was called 'a scouts'.

### scrammy weddings

When the groom and bride threw small change out of their 'going away' taxi or carriage to an assembly of small children. Deemed to be good luck. Sometimes known as 'hard up'. If no money was thrown it was called a 'scabby wedding'.

scouts

### scrapings

The small chips and pieces of fish and batter that floated around in a chip shop's deep-frier. They were continually scooped out and put in a compartment beside the frier. They were sold for around a penny a bag.

### scraps

Found in a book of 'scraps' or 'mottoes'. Usually girls gathered a 'set' by swapping with other girls. They were on various themes including angels, cherubs, poppy girls, wedding dresses, etc.

### scratcher

Somewhat impolite name for your bed.

### scrubbing boards

The corrugated board that was used to scrub the
dirt out of clothes. Eventually used by skiffle
groups (musical groups who improvised by using
odd items as instruments).

### scud

Perhaps you swam in the scud once? Bare naked!

scud

### see-sawing on gangways

While waiting on a boat or steamer, playing see-saw with a
gangway lying on the pier or wharf.

### seam o' teeth

Old dentures. Your grandparents may have had them but, as many
were ill-fitting, took them out between meals.

### semmits

The heavy vest much popular in earlier days. Together with
woollen drawers it made a 'woollen combination'.

### set-in beds

Boxed-in bed recess perhaps with a curtain across, in an alcove of
a wall in a bedroom or kitchen.

### shanks' naig or pony

When you were young this is the transport you mostly took …
you walked!

### shed

The parting on one side of your hair, though sometimes it was in
the middle of your head.

### sherrackin

What your mother or father gave you when you really annoyed
them. Usually accompanied by a skelp.

### sherbet dab

Sherbet in a wee bag with a lollie to dip in it.

### sheuch

Playing or sitting with your feet in the sheuch, the gutter. Was OK in the days before road congestion.

### shillings

One 20th of a pound in pre-decimal money. Also someone who was somewhat lacking up top was described as, 'not the full shilling'.

### shoogle

'Give it a wee shoogle' means to shake, push or nudge. The trams were called 'shooglies'.

### shove ha'penny

The football style game played on a table when pennies were used as players, and a ha'penny as the ball. The pennies were shoved by the hard edge of a comb or similar instrument, with each player having alternate shots.

### silver collection

At some special church events it was stipulated that only silver coins, as against copper coins, should be put in the collection plate.

### sine

Rinsing the dishes for your mother. Gave you an opportunity to have a 'skiddle' at the sink.

### single ends

A one-roomed apartment with no inside toilet where all family activity, including sleeping, took place.

### single lead soldiers

Very popular small toy soldiers, either painted or unpainted.

### sirens

The fearsome wail of the siren warned the population when there was the likelihood of enemy attack during World War Two. Also it signalled the 'all clear' when the threat had gone away.

### sithean

A hill that was reputed to be inhabited by fairies. Unfortunately when you went there, you never saw them.

### skarrach

A shower of rain that quickly passed and then the sun came out again.

### skelp

The smack you got when you did something wrong. No longer legal.

### skiddling at the sink

Wonderful entertainment for young children. Playing and splashing with water, bubbles and perhaps with wooden clothes' pegs or empty match boxes as boats.

### skiffing stanes

Small flat stones ideal for skiffing across the surface of a loch or the sea. The object was to see how many times it 'skiffed' or hopped through the water.

### skipping

'Cawing' ropes'. Making them go as fast as possible to make the jumper really have to move. Also singing various wee songs like:

*On a mountain stands a lady;*
*who she is I cannot tell.*
*All she wants is gold and silver,*
*all she wants is a fine young man in my ...*
then you called the next person to jump into the ropes.

Or there was:
*Vote, vote, vote for* [the name of the person who was skipping]
*In came* [the name of the next who came in at the beat] *at the door,*

*If it's* [the name of the local MP or councillor] *and his wife,
we'll stab them with a knife, and we don't want* [the person
skipping] *any more!*

Another alternative was:
*The big ship sails through the eellie alley o',
 the eellie alley o', the ellie alley o'.
The big ship sails through the ellie alley o',
on the last day of September.*

## skinnymalinkie

What you perhaps called very thin
people. As in the rhyme,
'Skinnymalinkie long-legs, big
banana feet.'

## skint knees

With so many children playing
outside, skint knees were the order
of the day. Having your mother
scrubbing the dirt out of a skint
knee could be painful.

## skiver

Someone who always avoids work,
a bit of a shirker. Probably
someone in your family who was
never to be seen when something
had to be done.

Skinnymalinkie

## skoosh

Skooshing water over someone from a bottle or water pistol.
Could be annoying, or if it was a very hot day, somewhat
refreshing. Mind you, if you went home soaking then you would
be in trouble.

### slates

Black school slates you wrote (or screeched) on with a slate pencil or charcoal or chalk. A sponge for rubbing out would be kept in an old tin. If the sponge was dry it would be spittle and cuffs that were used. Also provided was a sand tray, the same size as the slate, with a thin sprinkling of sand on its surface. It was to get you used to the rudiments of drawing and writing.

### sledging

Down hills, streets, pavements, anywhere there was a slope with snow on it, either on your sledge or tray.

### slice

Square Lorne sausage cut into slices. The traditional slice much loved by Scottish families.

### slider

Italian ice cream between two wafers. Nougats and double nougats were great favourites.

slider

### slides in the playground

During cold weather, ice-slides in school playgrounds were popular with pupils, though not with teachers or the jannie!

91

## slipper baths

Narrow baths in cubicles at a local authority swimming baths. You were provided with soap and a towel. The bath had two bolts as taps requiring an attendant's spanner to turn them on to fill the bath. This meant you couldn't lie there all day continually refilling the bath with hot water. The facility was used by some families who did not have a bathroom at home.

## sneck

The old latch, catch or snib on a door, that you quietly opened as you sneaked into the house.

## 'society man'

The insurance collector who called each week. Many families had 'penny policies'.

## sookin' rhubarb rock

Sweetie shaped like a stick of rhubarb. Could keep you going all day.

## soor plooms

Sour green balls of sweets, rather tart, which fairly drew your cheeks in!

## soot

Could be a hazard when cooking on the range, especially if someone had forgotten to put the lid on a pot, and soot was blown down the lum on a windy day (see 'chimney sweeps').

## soup

Your mother made the best. Usually with a piece of haugh, a knuckle bone or shank as its base, mixed with vegetables and pulses.

## soor dook cart

This came round the streets selling buttermilk, the liquid left over after producing butter from full-cream milk by a churning process. It was used in making bread, scones, creamy soups and sauces for boiled potatoes and cabbage.

### Spam

Chopped up bacon and pork. Famous for being in a can that required great skill to open without seriously damaging yourself.

### spangles

Packets of hard-boiled sweets. Could be obtained in various flavours.

### speaking only when you were spoken to

The rule in many a household, 'Children should be seen and not heard'.

### spinnie

Your granny's old spinning wheel. If still around it could be worth something!

### spoot-gun

A pop gun with a pump action. Something like a bicycle pump.

### spurtle

Wooden spoon used for stirring various foods including porridge. Or if you annoyed your mother she might threaten to give you a clout with it.

### stairheid

The landing in a tenement, lit at night. Up to six doors to various flats could lead off a stairheid. Famous for 'stairheid rammies' between neighbours. Impromptu 'stairheid concerts' were held, especially on rainy days, by children dressing up and performing little plays.

### stank

The grating covering a drain or cundy in a gutter. Many a good marble was lost down a stank!

### stappit fu

When you have eaten more than your fill, you are 'stappit fu'.

### steamer trips on the Clyde

Down the Clyde to Kirn, Dunoon, Innellan, Largs, the Kyles of
Bute, Arran, Tighnabruaich or Campbeltown, on a variety of
wonderful old Clyde steamers including *Glen Sannox, King George
V, Jeannie Deans, Duchess of Hamilton, Duchess of Rothesay,
Queen Mary, Caledonia, Mercury, Jupiter, Juno, Talisman,
Marchioness of Lorne and Marchioness of Graham.*

### steamie

The fondly remembered public laundry where people took their
dirty clothes to wash. Held a variety of sinks, cubicles and dryers.
Forerunner of the launderette. To be the 'talk of the steamie' was
to be the centre of gossip.

### sticky willy

The sprawling weed you threw onto your pal's clothes. It tended
to stick to you, so it wasn't easy to throw.

### stilts

Wooden stilts or, as a substitute, tin cans tied to
the feet. Great fun once you got the hang of it.

### stoater

Someone you admired or fancied, probably of
the opposite sex. 'Isn't he/she a big stoater!'

### stone ginger beer

Lemonade that came in brown clay bottles.
Would be kept in a cool place to give it an extra
edge.

### stookies

Plaster cast put on a broken limb, or if children
looked ill at ease, someone might say, 'Ye look
like a lot of stookies!'

### stovies

Sliced potatoes and onions stewed together
with a bit of meat. A favourite meal of
schoolchildren.

stilts

### streamers
Watching the Northern Lights or the Aurora Borealis streaming across the sky.

### string vests
Popular at one time but now only seen on the chest of Rab C. Nesbitt.

### 'stump ye?'
In poorer times, someone eating an apple could be surrounded by children shouting 'stump ye?' The first one to shout this got the stump of the apple to eat.

### sugarallie sticks
Small brittle sticks of liquorice for sucking.

### sugarallie-water
Pieces of liquorice in a bottle of water usually left under a bed for a week. Good for constipation but a poor substitute for lemonade. 'Sugarallie-water, black as the lum, save up yer pennies and you'll all get some'.

### Sunday school trips
Away for the day, perhaps on buses with streamers flying from the windows, then races and football in a park, followed by tea, and hot pies from long bakers' boards.

### sweetie bottles
Most sweets were unbagged and held in a large sweetie bottle in a 'sweetie-shop'. You could drive the assistant mad while you dithered about which ones you would choose, especially as she had to take them out and weigh them.

### sweetie cigarettes
Sweets that were shaped like cigarettes with red tips and were packaged with a football card inside. You swapped them to make a set. Imitating smoking gave you a 'grown-up' feeling.

## tablet

Solid fudge made from condensed milk, sugar and butter on a baking tray, and then cut up into squares. Most grannies made some.

## tackety boots

Popular boots with hobnail tacks protruding from the sole and sprigs at the heel and the toe. Made a terrible noise when you walked but great on ice slides in playgrounds.

## Tadpoles (powarts) in a jar

Found in a burn in late springtime, and taken home, much to the annoyance of parents.

## Take the High Road

The Scottish Television soap set in the fictional village of Glendarroch (actually Luss on Loch Lomond). It ran from 1980 until 2003. In 1995 the name was changed to just 'The High Road'.

## tammy troot

Popular character on children's radio, read by Willie Joss.

## tanners

The famous sixpenny piece coin. Forty of them made a pre-decimalization pound.

## tanner ba' players

Many famous Scottish football players were reputed to be good because as youths they were 'tanner ba' players'. In other words they played with a small rubber ball bought for a tanner (sixpence) with which they honed their skills.

### tattiebogle

Scruffy ragamuffin or scarecrow. 'Away an' get changed, you look like a right tattiebogle'.

### tattie howkin

Digging up potatoes. Hard back-breaking work for little money.

### tattie scones

Scones made with mashed potatoes, fat and flour and cooked on a griddle. A Scottish favourite to this day.

### tawse/the belt

The belt used in school to maintain discipline and dish out punishment. The popular one was a Lochgelly which left you with a very sore, stinging hand.

### tea-skiddle

A wee tea party for your friends.

### telegram boy

The boy on a bike who delivered the telegrams from the Post Office. Usually bad news!

### telling

Meaning to take heed of a warning. The teacher might say to you, 'You wouldn't take a telling, so you'll take the belt.'

### ten bob notes

The popular ten shilling (bob) note, the pre-decimalization currency that made you feel you had plenty of money.

### The Maggie

The film made in 1954, near Crinan, and on Islay, starring Paul Douglas and Roddy McMillan, with Tommy Kearins as 'the wee boy'. It told the story of an American businessman conned into shipping a valuable load of cargo to a Scottish Island on an old puffer.

## 'This is where we came in'

At the cinema it was usual for there to be an 'A' film (the big picture) and a 'B' film (the wee picture); both ran continuously. As people were allowed into the cinema during performances, it was noticeable that many people left when it came to the bit where they first started watching the film, hence the expression, 'this is where we came in'.

## 3D films and glasses

The glasses with red and green lenses were handed out at 3D films at the cinema. Remember ducking every time the Indians fired their arrows?

## thrupenny bits

Worth an 80th of a pre-decimalization pound, the popular nickel-brass twelve-sided thrupence was produced between 1937 and 1952. It ceased to be legal tender after August 1971. Silver thrupenny coins were introduced in 1551 and last produced in 1941.

## tick

Getting provisions on credit, usually until the next wage.

## tig

The game where you chased after someone, then when you touched (tigged) them you shouted 'Tig. You're het [hot]!', and they then became the chaser.

## tillie lamps

Oil-filled lamps used as auxiliary lighting along with gas.

## tin baths

Perhaps made of frosted zinc or galvanised steel, hung on the back of a door during the week and used for the weekly family bath night, usually on a Friday.

## tin cans

Empty ones were used as phones at the ends of a piece of string running from one can to the other and when pulled tight the voice at the other end could be heard. Or as stilts with string running through each can and held by the person on the stilt cans as they walked.

## toasting forks

They had extending handles to allow you to toast slices of bread held against the fire. Both sides had to be toasted individually and the results varied, but the smell was appetising.

## toddy

The mixture of whisky, sugar and hot water given when you had a cold.

## tonsils and adenoids

Having a tonsillectomy was common. Before the Second World War it could even be on the kitchen table! Jelly and ice-cream were the order of the day for a few days after the operation.

## toorie bunnets

Wee hats with bobbles on them, usually knitted by favourite aunties.

## tram cars

Tram cars were in Glasgow, Edinburgh, Aberdeen and Inverclyde. They usually had two decks, a 'current collector' sloping upwards pressed against the electrical cables above. The driver or motorman had two brass handles with which to control the tram. At the terminus the tram did not turn around. The conductress merely flipped over the backs of the seats like a set of dominoes.

### transfers

From a sheet of transfers or dabbities you selected one, moistened it, then stuck it onto your skin, probably the back of your hand. Next you peeled it back thus leaving the transfer.

### trench coats

Long raincoat. A relic of the First World War, worn by soldiers at the front. Good for covering you up on a cold day.

### trolley-buses

Buses that ran on an electrical current, with booms on top to catch the electricity from overhead wires. In Glasgow they only lasted for 18 years.

trolley bus

## uilie pig

The jar kept for oil in the press.

## Uncle Mac favourites

HELLO CHILDREN EVERYWHERE

Uncle Mac

Saturday morning children's favourites on the radio included the likes of 'Sparky and his lost voice', 'Nellie the Elephant' and 'Peter and the Wolf'. Uncle Mac, Derek McCulloch, was also the voice of 'Larry the Lamb' in 'Toytown'.

## unwrapped bread

Plain, unsliced bread with a large black crust, top and bottom. If newly baked, and you had been sent to the shops to get one, then the chances are you had a wee nibble at the outside before you got it home.

## vennel

An old lane or narrow alleyway with buildings on either side.

## wag-at-the-wa'

An inexpensive clock with the pendulum and weights exposed. The pendulum 'wagged' backwards and forwards. Much admired by children in their grandparent's home.

## wagon wheels

The popular large chocolate biscuit/treat with a creamy filling. Loved by schoolchildren for their 'playpiece'.

## walking to school

And probably getting soaked, so your coat was hung, steaming, over the radiator. It is said that the older you got the further you believed you had to walk to school!

## wally closes

Some tenement closes were either tiled, or half tiled, with glazed china tiles, many of exotic design. To live in a 'wally' close was seen as posh. In many wally closes only the entrance and the stair up to the first landing were tiled, after which it was just paint.

## wally dugs

Popular dog ornaments, usually a pair modelled on a King Charles spaniel. In many homes they sat one at either end of the mantelpiece.

## warts

Once very common on fingers and hands. You rubbed them with a potato to try to remove them or alternatively they could be frozen off by the nurse.

### wash-house boiler

The communal boiler, a large iron thing encased in a brick
structure with a coal fire underneath, had to be lit early in the
morning, so that the water would be at an appropriate
temperature when required. In the wash-house there were usually
two large sinks in which the washing could be rinsed. A large
stick or paddle was used to push the clothes into the hot water.
Tenants took their turn and the wash-house key was duly passed
from tenant to tenant. Sometimes the fire was lit by the 'man of
the house' before he went off to work.

### washing lines

A back court or back green, could be seen to be criss-crossed with
a number of washing lines as washing was put out to dry.
Disputes over whose turn it might be were a frequent cause of
arguments.

### wax-cloth

Similar to linoleum having the benefit of being hard wearing and
easy to clean. Cold to walk on with bare feet.

### wee cheese, wee butter

The game where two children, back to back with linked arms, lift
each other alternatively, one saying 'wee (weigh) cheese', the
other 'wee (weigh) butter'.

### weescule

The infant school, as opposed to the 'bigscule'.

### welly marks

The red welts/circles on your legs from the overwearing of
Wellingtons (topboots). If the socks fell down inside your wellies
you got the dreaded marks.

### whelks on a pin

Whelks from the seashore, boiled and eaten by picking them out
of their shell with a pin.

### wheesht

What your granny said when she wanted a bit of peace. 'Haud yer
wheesht!'

## Whisky Galore!

The 1949 film of the Compton MacKenzie novel about Scottish islanders who plundered 5,000 cases of whisky from a wrecked ship. It was based on the true story of the SS *Politician* which sank off Eriskay in 1941 with 250,000 bottles of whisky aboard.

## White Heather Club

The popular TV show which ran from 1958 to 1968. It was presented by Andy Stewart, who opened the show with the song, 'Come in, come in, it's nice tae see you ...'

Andy Stewart

## white pudding

A type of sausage filled with oatmeal, suet and onions.

## whigmaleerie

A trinket or ornament. 'Ma auntie has a whole lot of whigmaleeries on her mantelpiece'.

## whim wham

A pudding your granny made. A trifle with cream and orange.

## whistling

It seemed that most people could whistle popular tunes. It was not unusual to hear folks whistling as they walked down the street.

## wilkies

Tumbling o'er yer wilkies was rolling forward down a hill. Once you stood up you felt quite dizzy.

## winchin'

Going steady/courting.

## Windsor knots

A popular way of knotting a tie in the style created by the Duke of Windsor.

## winkle-pickers

The popular shoes with elongated pointed toes.

## wireless

In the early days of the 20th century, folks built their own 'crystal sets' that worked without any electrical power. It could be constructed from a piece of galena crystal, a safety pin and a wire connected to something iron and grounded on metal pipes. Detection of the radio signals came when you touched a wire (called the 'cat's whisker') to various points on the crystal.

'Listen, ah think ah've managed tae get some music on this set'
'Naw, ya daft laddie, it's the Salvation Army band coming up the street!'
Eventually crystal sets were replaced with four valve ones, which either worked off the mains or through wet or dry batteries.

## Woodbine

The cigarette of choice for many; tuppence for five, fourpence for ten or a single Wild Woodbine and a match for a ha'penny. Senior Service, Capstan, Craven 'A', Gold Flake and Players Navy Cut were also popular.

## wringers

Usually attached to a double sink where the clothes were wrung out by cawing the handle after washing.

## your mother's Co-operative number

Most people can remember it. You needed to use it to get the 'divi', the dividend, or pro-rata return on what your mother spent at the Co-op.

## your Sunday best outfit

In the days when most people went to church of a Sunday, a best suit/outfit was a necessity. Also used for weddings and funerals.